RENAISSANCE SOCIETY OF AMERICA REPRINT TEXTS 2

THE ITALIAN
RENAISSANCE

Edited by Werner L. Gundersheimer

Published by University of Toronto Press
Toronto Buffalo London
in association with the Renaissance Society of America

© Renaissance Society of America 1993
Printed in Canada

Reprinted 2002

ISBN 0-8020-7735-8

First published by Prentice Hall Inc. in 1965.
This edition reprinted by permission of Simon & Schuster Inc.

Canadian Cataloguing in Publication Data

Main entry under title:

The Italian Renaissance

(Renaissance Society of America reprint texts ; 2)
Co-published by the Renaissance Society of America.
Includes bibliographical references.
ISBN 0-8020-7735-8

1. Renaissance – Italy – Sources. 2. Italy –
Civilization – 1268–1559 – Sources. 3. Italy –
Intellectual life – 1268–1559 – Sources.
I. Gundersheimer, Werner L. II. Renaissance
Society of America. III. Series.

DG534.I73 1993   945'.05   C93-095002-X

FOREWORD

"The abbreviators of works do injury to knowledge and to love," says Leonardo da Vinci. They compose only "bald" works "fit for such impatient minds as conceive themselves to be wasting time when they spend it usefully in the study of nature and human things." This passage, which seems to damn this book and all similar enterprises, Dr. Gundersheimer has nonetheless bravely chosen as part of the final selection in the present volume. Even Leonardo might now despair at the mountain ranges of print that confront us all.

Far from intending injury to knowledge and love, far from catering to impatient minds, the editor of this volume has, with discrimination and affection, made it possible for all eager students of human things to take the first steps into a world of ideas now tantalizingly remote, and yet in many ways entirely familiar, to explore the period in history when these human things first began to compete with divine things for man's attention.

What should young men study? Of what use are the liberal arts? What can the ancients teach us? Why should we balance mental with physical exercise? How can a man devoted to lerning play an active part in society and politics? What can we learn from the careers of our great contemporaries? How do men in power actually behave and what lessons can we draw from their actions? How does man fit into the universe? The terms in which the men of fifteenth- and sixteenth-century Italy discussed these questions—which still agitate us powerfully—reflect their deep conviction that they were pioneers and innovators, repudiating their immediate forebears and moving forward boldly with the help of the long lost ancient thinkers whom they felt they had rediscovered.

But the editor does not limit himself to these humanist discussions of abstract problems, critically important though they are. He also shows us a trained humanist demolishing with vehemence a celebrated historical forgery. He gives us a humanist Pope's own account of his election to the Holy See. He even vouchsafes a glimpse of the scandalous behavior of some of the more notorious contemporary personages. In an occasional moving passage—for example that describing Nicolò Nicoli's disposition of his beloved library—we find ourselves in the actual presence of the men of the Renaissance.

Dr. Gundersheimer would be the first to rejoice if he should see the patient minds among his readers move from this volume of abbreviations to the texts themselves, and beyond. But we think this is a good beginning.

Robert Lee Wolff
Coolidge Professor of History
Harvard University

CONTENTS

INTRODUCTION

Few problems of interpretation of the history of Western civilization have persisted so long, become so complex, and so successfully resisted solution as has the problem of the Renaissance. The word *Renaissance* has come to be used in a variety of senses. For some scholars it denotes a movement of cultural revival based on ancient Greek and Roman models in literature, the arts, architecture, and political thought. For others it designates a period of rapid social, economic, cultural, and technological change, to which different scholars assign different chronological and geographical limits. Then, too, there have been those who would deny the validity of using the word *Renaissance* in any of these senses, or at all. Some maintain that the available evidence will not sustain the concept of a renaissance, whether as movement, period, or national efflorescence. Others hold that the interests and activities often associated with the Renaissance may also be found in an earlier period. Still others claim that the term is misleading because in one particular area of learning or another, they do not discern evidence of significant change. Thus, professional historians differ not only with respect to the problem of the Renaissance, but also with respect to the criteria by which the problem might be squarely met. Perhaps it is not so surprising that the most accomplished student of this problem, Wallace K. Ferguson, has recently chosen to write of *Europe in Transition, 1300-1520,* and has de-emphasized the "problem of the Renaissance" as such.[1] His view is that in the period roughly bounded by the years 1300 and 1600, Europe underwent a far-reaching transition from an essentially medieval to an essentially modern civilization. The rate of change

[1] (Cambridge, Mass.: Houghton Mifflin Co., 1963).

1

varied according to the place, the time, and the specific area of activity, but the result was an almost total change in the forms of art, thought, religion, and political, economic, and social organization. Professor Ferguson has traced the development of these changes in considerable detail, and his books make an ideal point of departure for a closer study of this problem.

The task of this book is modest: to present a small number of relatively extensive selections from documents which illustrate the life and thought of Italians in the fifteenth and early sixteenth centuries. The selections are intended to provide students and general readers with a broad sampling of the writings of educators, statesmen, philosophers, churchmen, and courtiers. In a society in which literacy was still the gift of a privileged minority, all these works were written for a very limited audience. There is little to be learned from them about the masses of peasants and urban laborers who surrounded every enclave of learning and civility. Therefore, they reflect little of the religion, art, and culture that was available for the overwhelming majority of Italian society in this period. Yet, most of the writers represented in this anthology may be considered humanists in some sense, and humanism is generally regarded as the dominant intellectual movement in Italy between Petrarch (1304-74) and Machiavelli (d.1527). Humanism, in any usual sense of the word, was the culture of an elite; but from the point of view of the cultural historian of this period, the only developments that can be thoroughly traced and analyzed occurred within the circles of this privileged minority. But *humanism* is a term second only to *Renaissance* in the number of interpretive problems it raises, and anyone who wishes to use either of them is obliged to attempt clear definitions.

The word *renaissance* means rebirth. The French word seems to have been applied to fifteenth-century Italy only in the nineteenth century, but various Italian writers from the fourteenth century on used metaphors of renewal, renovation, and rebirth to describe the cultural achievements of their own times. In fact, the basic idea of a renaissance is to a large extent a product of the way in which these writers thought of themselves and of their contemporaries in other fields. The notion of a middle time, between the ancient world and the present, a time in which one finds little but darkness and dissolution in learning, eloquence, poetry, and the visual arts, is a commonplace in the period under discussion. Petrarch, Boccaccio, Coluccio Salutati, Leonardo Bruni, and many others used it. Matteo Palmieri (1406-75), a Florentine writer, provides a typical example, during the 1430s:

> Where was the painter's art till Giotto tardily restored it? A caricature of the arts of human delineation! Sculpture and architecture, for long years sunk to the merest travesty of art, are only today in process of rescue from obscurity; only now are they being brought to a new pitch of perfection by men of genius and erudition. Of letters and liberal studies at large it would be best to be silent altogether. For these, the real guides to distinction in all the arts, the solid foundation of all civilization, have been lost to mankind for 800 years and more. It is but in our own day that men dare boast that they see the dawn of better things. For example, we owe it to our Leonardo Bruni that Latin, so long a bye-word for its uncouthness, has begun to shine forth in its ancient purity, its beauty, its majestic rhythm. Now, indeed, may every thoughtful spirit thank God that it has been permitted to him to be born in this new age, so full of hope and promise, which already rejoices in a greater array of nobly gifted souls than the world has seen in the thousand years that have preceded it.[2]

There is no doubt that many ambitious writers and artists viewed themselves as innovators during this period. Whether what they were trying to do was as new as they claimed, and whether the culture they hoped to supersede was as sterile as they alleged are separate questions, on which every informed student of the subject is entitled to form an opinion. But that they thought so, and managed to convince many succeeding generations, is a very important fact.

During this century, medievalists have made enormous contributions to our understanding of the thousand years that seemed so uniformly dark to Matteo Palmieri. We now have a very vivid appreciation for the originality and beauty of medieval art, a growing sensitivity to the vigor and complexity of political and social

---

[2] W. H. Woodward, *Studies in Education during the Age of the Renaissance* (Cambridge University Press, 1906), p. 67; quoted by D. Hay, *The Italian Renaissance in its Historical Background* (Cambridge: Cambridge University Press, 1961), p. 11.

institutions in the Middle Ages, and an increasing awareness of the sophistication and profundity of much medieval philosophy, theology, and science. As medieval studies have progressed, it has emerged quite clearly that the roots of many later developments may be found in the High Middle Ages (1000-1300), and that certain "medieval" cultural forms can be found even in the late sixteenth century. The old, somewhat exaggerated picture of the Renaissance as a drastic, abrupt departure from its immediate past has had to be greatly refined in the light of new evidence. Men of the Middle Ages were not so dull, credulous, and derivative, nor were men of the Renaissance so original, secular, and modern as the textbooks of an earlier generation suggest.

Yet, it is still widely believed that good reasons remain for using the term *Renaissance,* apart from its convenience as a customary label for a slice of historical time. The development of humanism in Italy between Petrarch and Machiavelli has often been cited in this connection. Neither the relevance of the excerpts here presented from renaissance authors, nor the relations between these authors can be properly understood without reference to the development of humanism.

Most people today think of a humanist as someone engaged in non-scientific studies, or committed to a kind of secularized religion of humanity. Since one of the traditional descriptions of the Renaissance is that of a gradual emancipation of the human spirit from medieval religiosity to modern secularism, this meaning of the word "humanism" has often been used or implied in discussions of the period. In order to understand what fifteenth- or sixteenth-century Italians meant when they referred to someone as a humanist (*humanista*), the modern reader must try to ignore the more recent meanings of the word. It was in the fifteenth century, according to Professor Paul O. Kristeller, that the word *humanista* appeared in the student slang of the Italian universities to denote a professor of the arts, the *studia humanitatis*.[3] These studies included grammar, rhetoric, poetry, history, and moral philosophy. Implicit in their treatment was the use of ancient authors, especially Romans, as sources of instruction and as models of eloquence and right

[3] Most recently, see *Eight Philosophers of the Italian Renaissance* (Stanford: Stanford University Press, 1964), pp. 3-5.

knowledge. Thus, Professor Kristeller has found the literal meaning of "humanism" in the Renaissance to be close to our term "the humanities." In his view, humanism can be identified not as an ideology, but as an educational program. This interpretation makes it possible for us to regard as humanists men who held widely differing beliefs and interests, who differed in their political and religious commitments.

What was the educational discipline of the humanists? How do we identify a humanist? Broadly speaking, the cultural context in which one finds humanists is that of a Christian society in which certain intellectuals are free to discover and study the pagan classics. The court of Charlemagne in the ninth century, and the cathedral school of Chartres in the twelfth century attracted a small group of men who were concerned with the study of the classics for their inherent interest and utility. In both of these cases, though, the available texts were relatively few in number, and often of lamentable quality. Moreover, the movement occurred within an extremely small society, and its consequences were not widely felt. These movements, though interesting, and important from the point of view of the transmission of ancient sources, were limited in scope, content, and social range. Only in Italy in the fourteenth century did humanism begin to have some effect upon a wider public of educated laymen from the upper classes.

The humanism of the Italian Renaissance was a product of an urban society. It gained the financial support, and often the active participation, of many of the mercantile, financial, hereditary, and clerical aristocrats. The humanists had easy access to an increasingly large and literate urban lay community, which possessed the leisure to enjoy culture, the social pretensions to desire it, the energies to nurture it, and the wealth to pay for it. But humanists and humanism only became marketable, so to speak, once they were generally known to be available. How humanism developed during the fourteenth century has been an important problem to students of the Renaissance.

It has often been assumed that humanism was originally and quite self-consciously created by Petrarch, whose love for the pagan classics stimulated him to formulate a negative conception of the Middle Ages, to attack the established system of scholastic education, and to popularize and celebrate ancient literature through propaganda and imitation. The work of recent scholars has shown that an interest in recovering, emending, and interpreting classical texts developed prior to Petrarch among the notaries and civil lawyers of the Italian city-states.[4] These men were entrusted with the duty of justifying the new independence of these territories according to traditions and precedents that antedated both the canon law of the Church and the customary and feudal traditions introduced by the invaders from the North. In their legal works, they sought to re-establish the Roman law, which they claimed had been corrupted over the centuries by barbarians. In their chronicles, they appealed to ideas of antiquity, and traditions of civic liberty and virtue. These imaginative conceptions of an ancient past were sometimes entirely without foundation, but the past was often earnestly searched as well as invented. History came to be used in a new way.

This link between humanism and jurisprudence seems even clearer when one considers that most of the celebrated early humanists were trained in legal studies. Petrarch is perhaps the most distinguished example. In succeeding generations, Coluccio Salutati and Leonardo Bruni, each the foremost humanist of his time, attempted to put both their legal training and their classical erudition and eloquence in the service of their civic ideals.

In Petrarch's thought, humanism was developed into a more specifically educational program. Petrarch gave the movement an offensive thrust by contrasting it with the academic philosophy of the universities. For varying lengths of time in different parts of Europe, humanists found it difficult to obtain professorships. The exclusiveness they often encountered, their own intransigence, and the rhetorical techniques which they culled from the ancient writings on eloquence helped to account for a rich literature of diatribes and invectives. Petrarch's "Of his own Ignorance and that of many Others" is the best early example of this literature.

By the early years of the fifteenth century, the revival of the classics had become a powerful instrument of change in several distinct areas. In literature, many humanists followed Petrarch in an attempt to model an elegant Latin style on Cicero's writings,

[4] N. Rubinstein, "The Beginnings of Political Thought in Florence," *Journal of the Warburg and Courtauld Institutes*, V (1942), 198-227.

some of which had been newly discovered. The forms of ancient literature—in biography, philosophy, history, poetry, *belles-lettres* —were studied and imitated. Some humanists, like Poggio Bracciolini, committed themselves passionately to the search for manuscripts. Others, like Bruni and Lorenzo Valla, prepared critical editions both of texts newly discovered and of others which they regarded as corrupted. The modern discipline of classical philology had its origins in the linguistic and historical criticism of humanist editors and commentators. Sound instruction in Greek became available as early as 1397, when a Byzantine scholar, Manuel Chrysoloras, gave his celebrated lectures in Florence. From that time on, many humanists studied with Greek and Byzantine scholars and prelates who traveled to the West, and a brave few headed eastward in search of instruction and manuscripts.

In education, the effects of the new classical revival were momentous. The educational treatises which constitute a large genre of humanist prose proclaim a new set of methods and goals. The *studia humanitatis,* not philosophy and theology, are stressed. The education of children is conceived as a preparation for a life of civic duty, pleasure in literature and in the arts, sports, and social gentility. The treatise by Petrus Paulus Vergerius, perhaps the first of its kind, reflects very clearly the values of the society for which he thought he could prepare the young. The success of Vergerius' treatise demonstrates that he had analyzed his audience correctly. The well-rounded Italian of Vergerius was modeled upon the well-educated Roman whom Cicero and Quintillian hoped to instruct. Both the Greek and Roman educational writers and their humanist successors were consulted by the influential schoolmasters who put humanist education to its practical test in the schooling of the young. The first humanist schools were begun by Vittorino da Feltre (1373-1446) at Mantua under the patronage of the Gonzaga court, and by Guarino of Verona (1374-1460) at Ferrara under the Este. Though few could benefit directly from these schools, they were widely imitated.

The influence of humanism is manifest in much of the art of the Italian Renaissance. The Roman architectural theorist Vitruvius was assiduously studied. Ancient theories of proportion, ancient structural techniques, ancient modes of decoration were admired, imitated, adapted. Sculptors turned to Roman sarcophagi for examples of classical art, and many went to Rome, pilgrims in search of relics from the past. The same influences were felt by many painters. In content, too, classicism became commonplace. Here humanists made their greatest contributions, by providing the thematic structure for a great deal of Renaissance painting. Alongside the conventional religious subject matter, one finds the art of humanism, in which classical form and classical content are fused into a vital, if somewhat nostalgic synthesis. Mythological and literary themes gained great favor, but historical subjects were also popular. A gradual secularization of subject matter is also evident in the development of portrait painting, of which the first known examples date from the 1430s.

Humanist political and historical thought is also of real importance. It has already been stated that the lawyers and notaries, in their search for authentic Italian secular legal traditions, turned to the study of the Roman law. In the fifteenth century, their efforts came to be affected increasingly by the philological techniques of literary humanism. Moreover their style, both as scholars and as public figures, became more securely modeled on ancient examples of political eloquence. A political leader in an Italian city-state had to be able to speak well in public, and there came to be a substantial demand for humanist rhetoricians. Some of the same kinds of influences were at work in historiography. The humanists conceived of history as a political narrative which had as its aims primarily the establishment of meaningful civic traditions, and the instruction of present leaders through examples drawn from the past. Many humanists took as their model the Roman historian Livy, who had the same civic and didactic concerns. Even a writer as profoundly original as Machiavelli may be considered a humanist, in the sense that he was both emotionally drawn to the study of the Roman past, and intellectually committed to teaching its supposed lessons to his readers.

In philosophy, a greatly expanded awareness of the ancient sources resulted from humanists' discoveries, editions, and commentaries. Though almost the entire body of Aristotle's extant writings had become known to Europeans during the thirteenth century, humanists continued to edit and discuss them. Their interests in literature, moral philosophy, and government led them to place great importance on works that had played a secondary role in the medieval curriculum, but the scientific, logical, and cosmological studies of Aristotle were not ignored. Many humanists, however, found the more literary philosophy of Plato to be most congenial with their own concerns, and hoped to found a new system, reconciling Christianity with a new Platonism based on the whole literature of ancient Platonic philosophy. This movement gained expression in Florence during the 1460s, when Cosimo de' Medici subsidized the labors of the young philosopher Marsilio Ficino, and enabled him to establish an informal center (misleadingly called an academy) for people interested in Platonic philosophy. This little community of Platonists came to exercise an influence out of all proportion to its size. Especially in literature and painting, to which Platonic theories of beauty and love offered a rich harvest of ideas and images, these themes became fashionable. The passage from Pietro Bembo's *Gli Asolani* presented here offers only one of many examples which might be found in the Italian, French, and English literature of the period 1475-1600. For Pico della Mirandola (1463-1494), the desire to reconcile apparently conflicting philosophies and theologies led to ambitious attempts at synthesis. A friend of Ficino's and a respected member of the Florentine circle, Pico hoped to discover the basic truths of all known systems of thought, an idea that may have been suggested, at least in part, by the abundance of newly discovered ancient sources.

It was no simple-minded propagandist, but rather the sober philosopher Ficino, who wrote, toward the end of the fifteenth century: "This is an age of gold, which has brought back to life the almost extinguished liberal disciplines of poetry, eloquence, painting, architecture, sculpture, and music. And all this at Florence." [5] Ficino could also have mentioned Milan, Venice, Naples, Rome, Urbino, Ferrara, Mantua, and a number of other centers where the efforts of enlightened patrons, humanistic scholars, and creative artists of all kinds combined to produce developments of lasting significance in the history of Western culture. The inven-

[5] W. K. Ferguson, *The Renaissance in Historical Thought* (Cambridge, Mass.: Houghton Mifflin Co., 1948), p. 28.

tion and spread of the art of printing from movable type enormously accelerated the rate of diffusion of humanistic culture, and helped to broaden the base of its appeal in the sixteenth century.

Despite its insistence on a return to the classical past in all fields of human activity, humanism was in a real sense an *avant garde* movement. Its programs challenged methods, attitudes, and assumptions that had long been accepted in the Church, in educational institutions, and among scholars and artists. Therefore, though this fact has sometimes been neglected by those who wish to present the Italian Renaissance as an age in which medieval culture was totally and definitively rejected, it is not surprising to find a strong conservative reaction against humanism and related movements.

For example, from the late thirteenth century on, there was in Italy a deep pietistic tradition that opposed the cosmopolitanism, the wealth, and worldly culture of the cities. St. Francis of Assisi was the first celebrated minister to the forgotten masses. He, and generations of his successors, carried their Christian message to a huge population which tried to subsist through famine, toil, oppression, and the countless wars and plagues which constitute the physical context of the Renaissance. St. Francis attempted, among other things, to dignify poverty. His successors, who carried on the tradition of public preaching, often outside churches, urged the reform of society as a whole. Such preachers are to be found throughout the fifteenth century. San Bernardino of Siena (1380-1444), one of the most influential, had so great a following that he was for a time regarded as a serious threat to the established Church. His sermons are models of pastoral admonition, simplicity, courage, and humor.

On a higher intellectual level, such prelates as Cardinal Dominici (1357-1419) engaged in polemics against noted humanists such as Salutati, and St. Antoninus (1389-1459), as archbishop of Florence, sought to reform the religious orders there, and to provide uplifting devotional works for his diocese. The popularity of such traditional piety is attested by the fact that at least one hundred editions of the latter's works were published before 1500. Girolamo Savonarola's (1452-1498) verbal and physical attacks on the luxury, elegance, and worldliness of Florentine life are justly famous for their considerable, if temporary, impact on the city. In a sense, though, he was simply a very traditional popular preacher, who for the most part worked within established genres of social and moral criticism.

In literature and the arts, powerful traditions coexisted with the innovations of humanists. For every painter who depicted subjects drawn from the pagan classics, or who attempted to imitate the style of the ancients, there was one who limited himself to the traditional religious iconography. The fifteenth century was not at all a secular age by present standards. The men who produced masterpieces of non-Christian art and literature were in general believing Christians, who did not view their professional activity as incompatible with their religious faith. It would have occurred to few, if any, of them to question seriously the existence of God, the immortality of the soul, the divinity of Christ, or any other fundamental doctrine of Christianity.

One historian of medieval thought, Etienne Gilson, has characterized the Italian Renaissance in negative terms; for him, it is essentially "the Middle Ages without God." [6] A fifteenth-century humanist would not have recognized this description of his own time. God, for him, would have seemed very much alive, and the Middle Ages would have receded beyond the horizon of history. In our picture, the lights and shadows will have to be softened somewhat. Humanism, in stressing the classics, made way for a new emphasis on the individual, on the dignity of man, and on human possibilities in general. The urban merchant societies, with their new social mobility, provided a practical counterpart to these theories, an arena in which they could be tested. The influence of both theory and practice is evident in secular literary and artistic developments. Though some people experienced history in a new way, and felt closer to men who lived fifteen centuries before than to those who lived five centuries before, all of these developments occurred within a general culture in which John of Salisbury or even St. Thomas Aquinas might have felt more or less at home much of the time.

The cities of Italy in the fifteenth and early sixteenth centuries were surely among the most exciting cities in western cultural his-

[6] F. Chabod, *Machiavelli and the Renaissance* (Cambridge, Mass.: Harvard University Press, 1958), pp. 221-222, provides references, and a brief summary of Gilson's position.

tory. To succeeding ages they left a priceless heritage of achievements in the arts, literature, classical scholarship, archeology, and
historical and political thought, as well as impressive contributions
in philosophy, economic theory and practice, and education. Yet,
we will be disappointed if we try to find in 1400 or 1500 a civilization in all respects different from that which existed in 1200 or
1300. As Federico Chabod, a great Italian scholar, has shown, continuity in culture is unavoidable, most change is very gradual, and
the new developments often occur within the formal framework
of the old systems, problems, and habits of thought. Thus, we must
look for change and development in the midst of continuity. Charles
Homer Haskins, the celebrated medievalist, was probably doing
precisely that when he stated his opinion that there was an Italian
Renaissance in the fourteenth and fifteenth centuries, "whatever
we choose to call it." [7]

In the following selections, some of the qualities and character-
istics of Italian life in this period will become evident, as will the
attitudes and assumptions of several of the keenest observers and
most articulate writers of an age in which eloquence was held in
high esteem.

[7] For Chabod's position, see his *Machiavelli and the Renaissance*, pp. 149-
200. Haskins' remark occurs in *The Renaissance of the Twelfth Century* (Cambridge, Mass.: Harvard University Press, 1928), p. 5.

℀ COLUCCIO SALUTATI

In 1374, at the age of 43, Coluccio Salutati arrived in Florence and began to work for the city as a notary. In the following year he was elected Chancellor, an office that he held through annual re-election until 1406, when he died. In a city ridden with internal factions and rivalries, he was universally trusted as a fair and loyal public servant. In addition, he became the leader and patron of the Florentine humanists. His arrival at Florence, in the year of Petrarch's death and the year before Boccaccio's death, provided a new standard-bearer for the stylistic and classical interests of their disciples. The elegance of his Latinity was legendary. Gian Galeazzo Visconti, the Duke of Milan who almost succeeded in subjugating the entire peninsula, is reported to have said that one letter of Salutati's did the Milanese cause more damage than a thousand Florentine horsemen; a voluminous diplomatic correspondence gives evidence of Salutati's gifts of eloquence.

Though Salutati subscribed to the conventional Christianity of his time, and was probably a man of genuine piety, he warmly supported the educational and literary innovations of the humanists. His reputation for piety and good judgment made him an excellent spokesman for the humanist cause, which he had several occasions to defend against attacks by conservative guardians of the scholastic curriculum. His replies usually took the form of letters addressed to an individual but intended for public circulation. Of these, the most important is his letter to a learned Dominican friar, Giovanni Dominici, who later became a cardinal.

Dominici (an influential popular preacher whose methods and influence have sometimes been compared with those of

13

Savonarola) had written a long treatise arguing that the study
of the liberal arts, including the Greek and Roman classics,
was not proper for children, and should only be granted to
learned adults under carefully controlled circumstances. In
his reply, Salutati considers the liberal arts individually, and
attempts to show that all of them are essential to the education of a Christian, as well as intrinsically valuable. The
excerpts which follow present his defenses of grammar, dialectic, and rhetoric, especially as these arts may be learned from
their ancient secular sources. It is interesting to note how
characteristically medieval much of Salutati's thinking is,
even when he is defending humanistic studies. (From *Humanism and Tyranny: Studies in the Italian Trecento,* by
Ephraim Emerton. Cambridge, Mass.: Harvard University
Press, 1925, pp. 246-61. Reprinted by permission of Harvard
University Press.)

From *A Letter in Defense of Liberal Studies*

I have read your book, reverend Father in Christ, and
find it a veritable splendor of noonday in which is no darkness at
all, and not, as you in your modesty call it, "A light shining in
the darkness." After the Prologue you give us forty-seven chapters,
following the letters of the passage you have chosen for your text
[*lux in tenebris lucet et tenebrae eam non comprehenderunt*],
truly an enormous work, in which you have gathered many excellent
selections and have displayed your vast learning to my great admiration.

Who would not marvel that so busy a man, continually occupied
with spiritual affairs, preaching to the people the word of God,
hearing and warning sinners in the secret of the confessional, speaking with God in prayer, hearing the voice of God as you read, soar-
ing, as it were, above yourself on wings of contemplation,—that a
man, I say, thus occupied, having scarcely time for the necessary
things of life, should have been able to put forth such a huge volume
merely to settle one little question! But, when we are led by the
goodness and the grace of God it is sure to happen that we can do
more than we supposed, nay, more than we could ask. He, that
Spirit which is above us, goes beyond us and does more than we his

instruments could accomplish. The limitless Supreme, though He works through us and in us, is surely not confined by any human measure. So that, whenever we see something done by a man which seems to be beyond ordinary human powers we can say, and we ought to confess and preach: "Lo! the finger of God is here!" Thus when we think of the lives of Augustine, Jerome, and Gregory, their work and their writings, we are amazed, our hearts fail us, and we say: "The Holy Spirit has done this, not these men."

So it is, venerable John, that I am all of a tremble at the very idea of speaking against you, and I dare not assail one single thing which you have established, not only because the finger of God has done it, but also because it seems utterly foolish to cast doubt upon what your learning and sanctity have laid down. When, however, I was reading your most elegant composition I came to the place where you sum up the whole controversy and raise the question whether it is right for Christian believers to make use of profane literature. I had already written to Brother John de Angelis who was persistently and absolutely denying that this was permissible to Christian men, and had said to him that it was necessary to the understanding of many books written by most holy doctors, Augustine, Jerome, and many others. I said also that when we are opposing the authority of the Gentiles, whether these be historians or poets, or, more dangerous still, orators or philosophers, we ought to be armed in every possible way. We did not, I said, put forward these studies and these traditions as an end in themselves, but as a means for going on to other things. Now everybody was saying that you maintain the very opposite of this opinion.

But—thanks be to God! who is the supreme and perfect Truth, from which as from a seed every true thing is derived—you say in the early part of your treatise, with admirable reasoning, precisely what I was saying. You set this forth at length and most cogently in your first twelve chapters. In the rest, however, you go on to a conclusion as if you were delivering a final judgment and putting an end to the whole question. You admit that the reading of profane literature is not to be forbidden to those who are instructed and established in the faith, as to which I never had any controversy with Brother John de Angelis. So that, if I chose to accept what you say, there would be nothing left for me to say in reply to

what comes afterward. But many have the impression that you
would like absolutely to forbid profane literature to Christians,
which I distinctly say ought not to be done, and to this you agree,
though only in part.

And indeed, most pious Sir, if you did not so earnestly place
nobility of intellect above the will, the very opposite of what I
maintained when I was discussing the nobility of law and medicine,
perhaps I would avoid the burden of a reply, giving way to your
authority and your reverend character. But, since it will be a help
to discuss this second point I will speak equally of both, so that
you may see whether I did well in placing the nobility of the intellect lower than that of the will, and whether we ought to say
that boys should not be initiated into profane literature, but should
begin with the study of the sacred writings. Then, after you have
seen what my opinion is on both these points, it shall be your part
to amend, to correct, to change, or to cut out whatever arguments
I shall put forth subject to your correction.

I will, then, begin with you, Reverend Father, a discussion, first
as to whether it is more satisfactory and more convenient to com-
mence our education with sacred literature or more useful to spend
some time on profane studies, and this shall be my first discussion
under six headings and shall form my first treatise. In the second
place we will consider whether I was right in giving to the will
precedence over the intellect, which seems not to be your opinion
nor that of great and holy authorities in your Order. When this
is done I will prepare a conclusion to the whole discussion, always
subject to the Truth, to better judgment and to your correction,
confident that, even though you remain of your present opinion,
still you will not despise one who thinks otherwise.

In this I shall proceed the more freely because I shall not make
any statement which in my opinion is an argument either for or
against the faith; but if this latter should happen I hereby now
revoke and condemn it. God has given his servant grace never to
have had a thought contrary to the faith. Even when human reason
seemed to contradict it I have never had the slightest hesitation.
How could my intellect venture to dissent from Holy Scripture or
be in doubt about that which has been settled by the whole body of
believers? I know not how it may be with others, but so it has al-

ways been with me. Even when I was a child and still more now, when with added years I have by God's grace seen and seriously considered more things, I have been most firmly convinced that no doctrine can be more compelling than our faith and the sacred writings; that whatever is contrary to these is utterly false and whatever departs from them is madness. I have always held it to be the greatest folly and intellectual presumption to deviate in any way from the precepts of Jesus, the teaching of Paul, the counsels given by both of them, the opinions and traditions of Jerome, the treatises of Ambrose, the expositions of Gregory and the discussion of Augustine or to disagree in any particular with men of such learning and holiness.

Let the mob of philosophers run after Aristotle or Plato or the pestilent Averroes or any better man if there is one—never mind about their names! I am satisfied with Jesus Christ alone, who while learning flourished in Greece and Italy and while Italy was crushing everything at her own pleasure by force of arms, "made foolish the wisdom of this world"—foolish, not through the wisdom of the wise nor the power of the strong, but through the foolishness of his preaching and his cross; through fishermen, not philosophers, through men of low estate, not those in worldly power.

And, since my first heading is the more important, being related to many things, as for instance to philosophers, grammarians, logicians, rhetoricians, and all the heathen who have handed down anything for us to learn, I will begin with Grammar which we know was in a high state of development before the time of Christ, and which is the gateway to all the liberal arts and to all learning, human and divine.

I

I have no doubt whatever that you will agree with me that those who are to enter upon the study of Christian doctrine must, by a kind of necessity, begin with Grammar. For, how can one who is ignorant of letters take in the knowledge of Holy Scripture? And how can one know letters without a knowledge of Grammar? Do you not see how ignorance of Grammar has misled monks and all who labor under the lack of such training? They do not understand what they read, nor can they properly present it to others for their reading.

A simple faith can, I admit, be perceived by the uneducated, but Holy Scripture and the commentaries and expositions of the learned they cannot understand. These can scarcely be comprehended by men of letters—I mean not those who have simply studied Grammar, but even those who have labored over Dialectics and Rhetoric. Grammar itself is in great part unintelligible without a knowledge of general facts [*rerum*], of how the essential nature of things changes, and how all the sciences work together—not to mention a knowledge of terminology. All studies in human affairs and in sacred subjects are bound together, and a knowledge of one subject is not possible without a sound and well-rounded education. But, however it may be with the ease or difficulty of learning Grammar, how about Christian doctrine itself? The Christian can with difficulty know just what he ought to believe, and if someone, on the authority of Scripture or of some reasoning however feeble, opposes him he will not know how to answer and will begin to waver in his faith. O, how many and what important questions do we hear every day which cannot be answered by mere crudity and a holy simplicity without the aid of learning! What would become of the whole body of the faithful if all were ignorant of letters or of Grammar? Of what avail would be the battle-line of believers against the heathen or against heretics without the learning supplied by Grammar, Logic, and Rhetoric?

Can any one deny that letters and Grammar were invented by the heathen and that, if those studies are to be forbidden to Christians, the art of Grammar itself will be closed to them? If this sounds absurd to us, why ought we entirely to reject the study of the heathen? Grammatical problems certainly cannot affect one's belief. The science of Grammar does not discuss and examine matters pertaining to the faith and to salvation, and therefore there is no danger in this kind of inquiry; no error hostile to the faith can thus be introduced. If sciences are to be rejected on account of their inventors—and it is a well known fact that they were all invented by heathen—why was it that the Christians accepted them from heathen hands? Why did they not all go to pieces? Why are they not condemned by everyone? Why are they taught and studied in your monasteries? Believe me, venerable John, it is neither fair nor reasonable to send into exile, as it were, the many teachings and traditions of the heathen, to exclude them from Christian homes, except insofar as they are opposed to the faith and to the conclusions of holy Fathers.

Nor do I think it fair, because one or another held a bad opinion of our faith, to proscribe the learning which he has handed down to us. The error of an author is one thing; the falseness or the contagion of the science he has invented is another. So that even if a heathen, a publican, a heretic, or a criminal has told the truth or professed a science harmless in itself, the truths he has spoken cannot be condemned on account of the fault of the author. . . .

The art of Grammar comes first in order and in [ease of] perception. It was, beyond all doubt, invented by heathen, whether we consider its discovery or its development. This we have to assume both from reason and from necessity, and, since we can acquire it from no other source than that from which it was derived, namely from the heathen, and since Christians, even though they have commented upon it, have most certainly taken all they say from the heathen, why do you forbid this and other studies for Christians?

Whence did the primitive Church learn how to express itself if not from the heritage of the heathen? When the call of God came to the nations and was accepted by them, how could they have learned to know the sacred writings and to understand their teachings and their purpose if they had been ignorant of their own learning, that is of Greek and Latin Grammar? Why do you cause this subject to be taught and studied in your own congregations and churches? On this point I think I have said enough, and I do not believe that you, when you have read the above, will deny its truth, in spite of what appears to be your absolute prohibition of profane studies to Christians.

Quintilian [c.35-95 A.D.; Roman authority on eloquence] says, if I may very briefly quote his own words, that this science is divided into two parts, the art of correct speech and the interpretation of the poets, and hence it has more in reserve than is shown on the surface. And farther on he says:

It is not enough to have read the poets; every kind of writing should be studied carefully, not only for the contents, but also for the words, which often derive their force from the authors who use them. Grammar is incomplete without music, when we have to speak of meter and rhythm. If it be ignorant of astronomy it cannot understand the poets who, not to mention other things, are continually making use of the rising and setting of the constellations in their descriptions of time. Nor can it ignore philosophy on account of the numerous passages in almost all poems drawn from an intimate familiarity with the philosophy of Nature [i.e., natural science], as, e.g., Empedocles among the Greeks and Varro and Lucretius among the Latins, who delivered their message of wisdom in verse. Furthermore we need no small degree of eloquence if we would speak fully and appropriately of each proposition we have demonstrated.

When Fabius [Quintilian] had said this, he added:

Wherefore those persons are not to be tolerated who criticize this science as trifling and vacant, for unless it has laid solid foundations for the future orator, whatever he builds thereon will fall to the ground. It is a necessity for youth, a joy to the aged, a sweet companion in solitude, the only element in every form of study which has more of utility than of display.

Thus M. Fabius Quintilianus, that most highly cultivated writer, in the first book of his *Institutes of Oratory*.

To this should be added, in order to show the wide scope of this discipline, the work of Marcianus Mineus Felix Capella, in which, after the first two books describing the marriage of Philology and Mercury, he sets forth with the perfection of brevity the doctrine of the seven liberal arts.

So that, since it is the function of Grammar to know these arts and to teach them, and since this branch of learning should precede all others, and since it is a part of the heritage of the Nations, it follows logically and of necessity that, far from being prohibited to Christians, it ought to be placed before all other studies. But of this I have spoken elsewhere; and now, having said enough about Grammar we will go on to Logic.

II

Who can deny that Dialectics, being an inquiry after truth, which is the sole object of all liberal arts and of every science, is a necessary study for Christian men? Our faith is the supreme Truth, and we come to it through truths without number. Since then this science is the instrument for discovering and estimating truth, who cannot see that it is a necessity to Christian believers in reaching the goal of Christian truth? Shall not the believer begin by learning first the substance of the faith, and then, after he has made a habit of this, as you would have him do, turn to the studies by which he may comprehend and defend what he has already perceived?

Tell me, my venerable John, when can any one be fortified on every side in purity of faith by human reason unless he reach this truth through the discussion of those endless doubts by which it is wont to be weakened and through knowing and removing many arguments on one side and the other? It is most true, as Democritus, quoted by Cicero, said, that Nature has hidden the truth in deepest mystery. So that, if Nature has hidden her truths, that is, natural truths—for he knew of no others—in such depths, what shall we think of that infinite power whose nature is such that we do well to call it supernatural?—especially since the truths of Nature are finite, while this power must be acknowledged as infinite. In what depth, what pit, what abyss does supernatural truth lie concealed!

But now, the things we hold by faith alone being of such a nature that natural reason cannot reach them, it is easy for some fiction of human reasoning to shake them from the place they once held. Therefore it is necessary for neophytes to learn, together with the doctrine, the means by which to defend it. Who would allow raw recruits, untrained in military affairs, without teaching in the principles of war, to be placed at the post of danger unarmed and not even knowing with what weapons to defend themselves or to attack the enemy? With what reason could they be used even in a slight skirmish? Let them learn at one and the same time to handle weapons, to fight, to conquer and to meet danger, lest at the first encounter they should be struck with terror and beat a retreat or, if they cannot escape, should be captured.

So much for Logic, which acts on the intellect with compelling force by means of reasoning. Now let us pass on to Rhetoric which accompanies Logic, but acts upon the will. Both of these aim at the same goal but by different ways. The one enlightens the mind to an intellectual conviction; the other brings it into a willing attitude, or, to put it in another way, the one proves in order to teach; the other persuades in order to guide.

III

I know not how to carry on this discussion more effectively than by using the words of Saint . . . Augustine. In the fourth book of his *De Doctrina Christiana* he solves the problem as follows:

> The art of Rhetoric may be used to persuade both to truth and to falsehood, and who dare say that the truth (in the person of its defenders) ought to stand unarmed against falsehood so that those who are trying to persuade men to falsehood shall know how to make their audience friendly and interested and receptive from the start, while the champions of truth shall not know how to do this? Shall the former present falsehood tersely, clearly, and plausibly while the latter set forth the truth so that it is tedious to hear, difficult to understand, and unattractive to believe? Are the former to oppose truth with fallacious arguments and false assertions, while the latter are unable to defend the truth or to refute falsehood? Shall the former stir the minds of their hearers to error, terrify, sadden, rouse, and exhort in glowing speech, while the latter are cold, slow, and languid in the defense of truth? Who is such a fool as to call this wisdom? Since, then, the art of eloquence standing between the two can persuade powerfully to either good or evil, why is no preparation made by good men to fight for the truth when evil men are using this art in the service of wrong or error to gain their own vain and wicked ends?

Such are the words of the holy father Augustine. And now, then! Does it really seem to you that this famous doctor is forbidding to Christians and to those entering upon the way of God the study of

Rhetoric, although it is the heritage of Cicero, the special weapon of the heathen, their sword and spear? He saw in others and felt in himself how easily scholars allow Grammar, Logic, and Rhetoric to make their way into theological truth. He saw how necessary these are to beginners in order to learn and to understand the sacred writings. He remembered what a protection they were to him when he had fallen into the Manichaean heresy, how they had saved him from remaining, through ignorance, in the error in which he had been caught. He did not forget that the first glory of his salvation flashed upon him out of the darkness of Cicero, the man whose language, as he himself says, was admired by almost everyone—not so, however, his soul!

> That book of his called *Hortensius* contains an exhortation to philosophy, and yet that book changed my whole attitude of mind and caused my prayers to turn to thee, O Lord, and changed my will and my desire. The whole vain show became suddenly a vile thing to me, I desired immortal wisdom with an incredible longing of the heart, and I began to arise and return to thee.

All this Father Augustine said, and here you can see what fruit our God, Creator and Redeemer, drew from out the filthy rubbish of the heathen. So Augustine could not have taught that Christians should be prohibited from things which he remembered by the grace of God to his own salvation, things which he knew were not merely an instrument but a summary of many truths and which he had found a wall of defense for the truth, a weapon, a tool and a sword of protection and victory when he had to fight for the faith or for the sacred writings. Who amid the audience of scholars would desire the banishment of teaching by which he was profiting every day and making progress more and more toward the truth he was seeking?

Imagine for yourself a person well grounded in the *trivium,* that is, in the literary studies; then let him enter on the study of Christian doctrine and sacred literature at the same time with another person untrained in those [preliminary] branches, and which do you think would or ought to become steeped [in sacred learning] the more rapidly, or the more completely, the trained man, or the crude and ignorant one? Finally, since the whole *trivium* is a way and a means, not an end, and is planned so that through it we become able to learn other things and not that we may rest in it, is it not a preposterous and utterly ridiculous idea after the end has been reached to go back and work around to the goal again? If, as you would have it, after we have learned what pertains to the faith and have become well grounded therein, these [literary] subjects are to be studied, tell me, I pray you, to what end? Is it for their own sakes? But they are not an end in themselves. Is it that we may progress further? But we shall already have passed the boundary and left behind us the final goal of all learning!

I can see no reason for this opinion, my dear John, unless it were that, finding you have not reached your goal, you follow the example of men who have lost their way and have strayed from the true, straight, and well-worn path and so you turn back to the point at which you wandered away. But enough of this! . . .

PETRUS PAULUS VERGERIUS, *The Elder*

Even the simplest circumstances of Vergerius' life have been much disputed, but it is now generally accepted that he was born in Capo d'Istria in 1370, and died in Budapest in 1444. He was educated in Padua and Florence, where he studied Greek under the great Byzantine scholar Manuel Chrysoloras. He appears to have been a doctor of law, medicine, and philosophy, and he served for some years as professor of logic in the University of Padua. He was familiar with the major intellectual developments of his time, and accepted elements of both humanism and scholasticism. After 1405, Vergerius became increasingly involved in ecclesiastical questions, and played an active role at the councils of Constance and Basle. He then entered the service of the Emperor, in which he seems to have remained for the rest of his life.

The treatise *De Ingenuis Moribus* ("concerning excellent traits") probably was written between 1400 and 1402. Not only one of the first educational treatises produced by a humanist writer, it was also one of the most influential. It survives in many manuscripts, went through many printed editions, and was widely known and respected well into the sixteenth century. The work is addressed to Ubertinus, the young son of Francesco Carrara, the lord of Padua, and it succinctly summarizes the educational ideals that came to be fostered in the humanistic schools attached to Northern Italian princely courts during this period. Many of the characteristic themes of humanist educational thought emerge here—the relationship of arms and learning, the importance of physical as well as mental development, the need for a familiarity with all of the liberal arts. Vergerius often uses classical authors to support his views, and is clearly interested in recapturing the achievements of Greek and Roman education. His concern for the moral qualities of the young is also very striking.

It is interesting to note that the selection ends with an attempt to resolve the question of the relationship between the lives of action and contemplation. Here, civic ideals emerge as Vergerius states that "the man who has surrendered himself absolutely to the attraction of Letters or of speculative thought follows, perhaps, a self-regarding end and is useless as a citizen or as prince." Here the very practical concerns of the humanist in a city-state appear. Vergerius calls for the well-rounded individual of high attainments, and tries to show how such men may be developed. (From *Vittorino da Feltre and Other Humanist Educators,* by William Harrison Woodward. London: Cambridge University Press, 1897, pp. 96-110. Reprinted by permission of Cambridge University Press.)

P. P. Vergerius to Ubertinus of Carrara

1. Your grandfather, Francesco I, a man distinguished for his capacity in affairs and for his sound judgment, was in the habit of saying that a parent owes three duties to his children. The first of these is to bestow upon them names of which they need not feel ashamed. For not seldom, out of caprice, or even indifference, or perhaps from a wish to perpetuate a family name, a father in naming his child inflicts upon him a misfortune which clings to him for life. The second obligation is this: to provide that his child be brought up in a city of distinction, for this not only concerns his future self-respect, but is closely connected with the third and most important care which is due from father to son. This is the duty of seeing that he be trained in sound learning. For no wealth, no possible security against the future, can be compared with the gift of an education in grave and liberal studies. By them a man may win distinction for the most modest name, and bring honor to the city of his birth however obscure it may be. But we must remember that while a man may escape from the burden of an unlucky name, or from the contempt attaching to a city of no

repute, by changing the one or quitting the other, he can never remedy the neglect of early education. The foundation, therefore, of this last must be laid in the first years of life, the disposition molded while it is susceptible, and the mind trained while it is retentive.

This duty, common indeed to all parents, is specially incumbent upon such as hold high station. For the lives of men of position are passed, as it were, in public view; and are fairly expected to serve as witness to personal merit and capacity on part of those who occupy such exceptional place among their fellow men. You therefore, Ubertinus, the bearer of an illustrious name, the representative of a house for many generations sovereign in our ancient and most learned city of Padua, are peculiarly concerned in attaining this excellence in learning of which we speak. Our name, our birthplace, are not of our own choice. Progress in learning, on the other hand, as in character, depends largely on ourselves, and brings with it its own abiding reward. But I know that I am urging one who needs no spur. Can I say more than this?—continue as you have begun; let the promise of the future be consistent with your performance in the past.

To you, therefore, I have addressed this tractate upon the principles of Learning and of Conduct: by which I intend the subjects and the manner of study in which youth may be best exercised, and the actions which it behooves them to pursue, or to avoid, in the course of their daily life. Although addressed to you, it is intended for all who, blessed by nature with quickened minds and lofty aims. desire to show by their lives their gratitude for such gifts. For no liberal mind will readily sink into mere sloth or become absorbed in the meaner side of existence.

2. In *judging character* in youth, we recognize, first of all, that it is a mark of soundness in a boy's nature that he is spurred by desire of praise: upon this rests Emulation, which may be defined as rivalry without malice. Next we notice the quality of willing and ready obedience, which in itself is full of promise for future progress, while, combined with the love of approbation, it suggests the possibility of the highest excellence. For, as yet, the boy is not of an age to be stimulated by the dictates of reason, which would

be, doubtless (as Plato and Cicero said), the surest motive, but Emulation, going along with obedience, supplies that which reason is as yet too weak to give. Again, we prize every sign of alertness, of industry, of thoroughness, in the growing character. As in a horse the mettle which needs neither whip nor spur, so in a boy eagerness for learning marks a temper from which much may be hoped. Where all these qualities are found united we need have little anxiety as to character at large. Again, we may feel confidently about a boy who shows signs of due shame at punishment or disgrace, or who respects his master in spite of it. The boy, too, who is naturally of a friendly disposition, forgiving, sociable, taking all that is said and done in good part, gives good promise for the future. Perhaps we may add, with Aristotle, that excessive physical energy rarely goes with keen intellectual tastes. Arguments drawn from physiognomy I prefer to leave to others. But we have said enough to show how bent of character may be recognized in early years. And we may admit that there is often a relation between dignity of mien and loftiness of temper. Socrates suggested that boys should be encouraged to regard themselves in a mirror, that the boy of dignified bearing may feel himself bound to act worthily of it, the boy of less attractive form braced to attain an inner harmony to compensate for his defect. Perhaps, however, we gain surer stimulus from contemplating others than from the reflection of our own selves: as Scipio, Fabius, and Caesar kept before their eyes the images of Alexander or other heroes of the past.

If, however, it is helpful to contemplate the outward form of a dead hero, how much more shall we gain from the example of living worth? For it is with character as with instruction: the "living voice" is of far more avail than the written letter; the life we can observe, the character actually before us, affect us as no other influence can. Let, then, the examples of living men, known and respected for their worth, be held up for a boy's imitation. And, moreover, let those of us who are older not forget so to live that our actions may be a worthy model for the youth who look up to us for guidance and example.

As to the *moral discipline* of the young, we must remember, first, that each age has its peculiar dangers, and next that these are due in part to natural bent, in part to defective training or to inexperience of life. For instance, a boy will be of open-handed and generous disposition, just as he is by virtue of his years of warm and sanguine habit of body: and such a temper we prefer to parsimoniousness. But yet a habit of squandering money thoughtlessly, from indifference to its value, or carelessness as to the character of those upon whom it is bestowed, must be checked. Again, the same superabundant vitality which, rightly directed, inspires a young man to high endeavor, may, without such guidance, generate a spirit of arrogance, or intolerable self-conceit. Herein lies that great danger to character, a habit of boasting, which in turn gives rise to a disregard of truth in all relations of life, a fault apt to become ingrained as years roll by. Nothing so injures a young man in the eyes of serious people as exaggeration and untruthfulness. Indeed a master will be well-advised to inculcate generally a habit of speaking little, and seldom, and of answering questions rather than asking them. For a youth who is silent commits at most but one fault, that he is silent; one who is talkative probably commits fifty. Looseness of conversation must be vigorously dealt with, remembering the poet's warning, repeated by St. Paul: the natural sense of shame may be successfully appealed to in this matter. Once more, if boys are credulous we may ascribe it to inexperience; if they change their tastes or opinions, it is due to the flux of the bodily humors, caused by excess of natural heat. This, moreover, produces also that intensity or passion in all that they do which scarcely admits of precepts of moderation, and certainly not of harsh condemnation, for it belongs to their age, and has its proper function in early years. To this same natural tendency we may attribute the fickle character of their first friendships.

Children, although for the most part under the unwritten discipline of home, are not to be regarded as outside the control of public regulation. For the education of children is a matter of more than private interest; it concerns the State, which indeed regards the right training of the young as, in certain aspects, within its proper sphere. I would wish to see this responsibility extended. But to come to detail. It is especially necessary to guard the young from the temptations natural to their age. For, as has been said, every period of life has its own besetting sins. Manhood is the age of passion, middle-life of ambition, old age of avarice. I speak, of course, in general terms. So, too, we find faults common to boyhood, which are obvious subject for regulations. In order to maintain a high standard of purity all enticements of dancing, or suggestive spectacles, should be kept at a distance: and the society of women as a rule carefully avoided. A bad companion may wreck the character. Idleness of mind and body is a common source of temptation to indulgence, and unsociable, solitary temper must be disciplined, and on no account encouraged. Harmful imaginations in some, moroseness and depression in others, result from want of healthy companionship. Tutors and comrades alike should be chosen from among those likely to bring out the best qualities, to attract by good example, and to repress the first signs of evil. All excess in eating and drinking, or in sleep, is to be repressed: though we must not forget the differing needs of individuals. But our physical nature should be satisfied only, not pampered. In the matter of allowing wine to children I should prohibit its use, except in the smallest quantities, and even then carefully diluted, with water in the larger proportion. But in no case is it allowable to eat, drink, or sleep up to the point of complete satisfaction; in all bodily pleasures we must accustom our children to retain complete and easy control of appetite.

Above all, respect for Divine ordinances is of the deepest importance; it should be inculcated from the earliest years. This reverential temper, however, must not be forced in such a way that it pass into unreasoning superstition, which engenders contempt rather than faith. Profane language is to be held an abominable sin; and disrespect toward the ceremonies of the Church or vain swearing must be sternly repressed. Reverence toward elders and parents is an obligation closely akin. In this, antiquity offers us a beautiful illustration. For the youth of Rome used to escort the Senators, the Fathers of the City, to the Senate House: and awaiting them at the entrance, accompany them at the close of their deliberations on their return to their homes. In this the Romans saw an admirable training in endurance and in patience. This same quality of reverence will imply courtesy toward guests, suitable greetings to elders, to friends, and to inferiors. For right bearing in these points is always attractive; and in none more than in the son of a Prince, who must unite in his carriage a certain dignity with a becoming and natural ease.

And these details of personal bearing can be learned by observation, aided by wise guidance. This, indeed, must often take the form of correction, and will, perhaps, be most needed by those who are to be called to the sovereignty of a city or a state. The reproofs of our friends may be likened to a faithful mirror: and he who willfully refuses to listen to them flings himself thereby into the arms of flatterers. For it is little short of a miracle that a man of wealth, of birth and of station, brought up amid luxury and ease, should prove himself on all occasions wise and strong; the allurements of pleasure, and the evil influence of parasites, with every opportunity of self-indulgence, leave scarcely a chink by which reason and integrity may force an entrance. Plato, in the *Gorgias,* specially commends the man who in such surroundings can resist temptation. I would have you note that one special source of danger lies in the weak indulgence of parents, which undermines the moral strength of their children; and this is often seen the more conspicuously when the father's stronger hand has been taken away. Therefore I strongly approve of the system under which children liable to such dangers are educated abroad; or if in their own city, in the house of relatives or friends. For as a rule the sense that they are not in their own house checks self-will and imposes a healthy restraint upon boys, and removes, at least, some of the hindrances which stand between them and full devotion to those liberal studies which I must now set forth.

3. We call those studies *liberal* which are worthy of a free man; those studies by which we attain and practice virtue and wisdom; that education which calls forth, trains, and develops those highest gifts of body and of mind which ennoble men, and which are rightly judged to rank next in dignity to virtue only. For to a vulgar temper gain and pleasure are the one aim of existence, to a lofty nature, moral worth and fame. It is, then, of the highest importance that even from infancy this aim, this effort, should constantly be kept alive in growing minds. For I may affirm with fullest conviction that we shall not have attained wisdom in our later years unless in

our earliest we have sincerely entered on its search. Nor may we for a moment admit, with the unthinking crowd, that those who give early promise fail in subsequent fulfillment. This may, partly from physical causes, happen in exceptional cases. But there is no doubt that nature has endowed some children with so keen, so ready an intelligence, that without serious effort they attain to a notable power of reasoning and conversing upon grave and lofty subjects, and by aid of right guidance and sound learning reach in manhood the highest distinction. On the other hand, children of modest powers demand even more attention, that their natural defects may be supplied by art. But all alike must in those early years,

Dum faciles animi iuvenum, dum mobilis aetas,

while the mind is supple, be inured to the toil and effort of learning. Not that education, in the broad sense, is exclusively the concern of youth. Did not Cato think it honorable to learn Greek in later life? Did not Socrates, greatest of philosophers, compel his aged fingers to the lute?

Our youth of today, it is to be feared, is backward to learn: studies are accounted irksome. Boys hardly weaned begin to claim their own way, at a time when every art should be employed to bring them under control and attract them to grave studies. The Master must judge how far he can rely upon emulation, rewards, encouragement; how far he must have recourse to sterner measures. Too much leniency is objectionable; so also is too great severity, for we must avoid all that terrifies a boy. In certain temperaments —those in which a dark complexion denotes a quiet but strong personality—restraint must be cautiously applied. Boys of this type are mostly highly gifted and can bear a gentle hand. Not seldom it happens that a finely tempered nature is thwarted by circumstances, such as poverty at home, which compels a promising youth to forsake learning for trade: though, on the other hand, poverty is less dangerous to lofty instincts than great wealth. Or again, parents encourage their sons to follow a career traditional in their family, which may divert them from liberal studies: and the customary pursuits of the city in which we dwell exercise a decided influence on our choice. So that we may say that a perfectly unbiased decision in these matters is seldom possible, except to certain select natures, who by favor of the gods, as the poets have it, are unconsciously brought to choose the right path in life. The myth of Hercules, who, in the solitude of his wanderings, learned to accept the strenuous life and to reject the way of self-indulgence, and so attain the highest, is the significant setting of this profound truth. For us it is the best that can befall, that either the circumstances of our life, or the guidance and exhortations of those in charge of us, should mold our natures while they are still plastic.

In your own case, Ubertinus, you had before you the choice of training in Arms or in Letters. Either holds a place of distinction among the pursuits which appeal to men of noble spirit; either leads to fame and honor in the world. It would have been natural that you, the scion of a House ennobled by its prowess in arms, should have been content to accept your father's permission to devote yourself wholly to that discipline. But to your great credit you elected to become proficient in both alike: to add to the career of Arms traditional in your family, an equal success in that other great discipline of mind and character, the study of Literature.

There was courage in your choice. For we cannot deny that there is still a horde—as I must call them—of people who, like Licinius the Emperor, denounce learning and the Arts as a danger to the State and hateful in themselves. In reality the very opposite is the truth. However, as we look back upon history we cannot deny that learning by no means expels wickedness, but may be indeed an additional instrument for evil in the hands of the corrupt. To a man of virtuous instincts knowledge is a help and an adornment; to a Claudius or a Nero it was a means of refinement in cruelty or in folly. On the other hand, your grandfather, Jacopo da Carrara, who, though a patron of learning, was not himself versed in Letters, died regretting that opportunity of acquiring a knowledge of higher studies had not been given him in youth; which shows us that, although we may in old age long for it, only in early years can we be sure of attaining that learning which we desire. So that it is no light motive to youthful diligence that we thereby provide ourselves with precious advantages against on-coming age, a spring of interest for a leisured life, a recreation for a busy one.

Consider the necessity of the literary art to one immersed in reading and speculation, and its importance to one absorbed in affairs. To be able to speak and write with elegance is no slight advantage in negotiation, whether in public or private concerns. Especially in administration of the State, when intervals of rest and privacy are accorded to a prince, how must he value those means of occupying them wisely which the knowledge of literature affords to him! Think of Domitian: son of Vespasian though he was, and brother of Titus, he was driven to occupy his leisure by *killing flies!* What a warning is here conveyed of the critical judgments which posterity passes upon Princes! They live in a light in which nothing can long remain hid. Contrast with this the saying of Scipio: "Never am I less idle, less solitary, than when to outward seeming I am doing nothing or am alone": evidence of a noble temper, worthy to be placed beside that recorded practice of Cato, who, amid the tedious business of the Senate, could withdraw himself from outward distractions and find himself truly alone in the companionship of his books.

Indeed the power which good books have of diverting our thoughts from unworthy or distressing themes is another support to my argument for the study of Letters. Add to this their helpfulness on those occasions when we find ourselves alone, without companions and without preoccupations—what can we do better than gather our books around us? In them we see unfolded before us vast stores of knowledge, for our delight, it may be, or for our inspiration. In them are contained the records of the great achievements of men; the wonders of Nature; the works of Providence in the past, the key to her secrets of the future. And, most important of all, this knowledge is not liable to decay. With a picture, an inscription, a coin, books share a kind of immortality. In all these memory is, as it were, made permanent; although, in its freedom from accidental risks, literature surpasses every other form of record.

Literature indeed exhibits not facts alone, but thoughts, and their expression. Provided such thoughts be worthy, and worthily expressed, we feel assured that they will not die: although I do not think that thoughts without style will be likely to attract much notice or secure a sure survival. What greater charm can life offer than this power of making the past, the present, and even the future our own by means of literature? How bright a household is the family of books! we may cry, with Cicero. In their company is no noise, no greed, no self-will: at a word they speak to you, at a word they are still: to all our requests their response is ever ready and to the point. Books indeed are a higher—a wider, more tenacious —memory, a store-house which is the common property of us all.

I attach great weight to the duty of handing down this priceless treasure to our sons unimpaired by any carelessness on our part. How many are the gaps which the ignorance of past ages has wilfully caused in the long and noble roll of writers! Books—in part or in their entirety—have been allowed to perish. What remains of others is often sorely corrupt, mutilated, or imperfect. It is hard that no slight portion of the history of Rome is only to be known through the labors of one writing in the Greek language [Polybius, c.205-c.123 B.C.]: it is still worse that this same noble tongue, once well-nigh the daily speech of our race, as familiar as the Latin language itself, is on the point of perishing even among its own sons, and to us Italians is already utterly lost, unless we except one or two who in our time are tardily endeavoring to rescue something —if it be only a mere echo of it—from oblivion.

We come now to the consideration of the various subjects which may rightly be included under the name of "Liberal Studies." Amongst these I accord the first place to History, on grounds both of its attractiveness and of its utility, qualities which appeal equally to the scholar and to the statesman. Next in importance ranks Moral Philosophy, which indeed is, in a peculiar sense, a "Liberal Art," in that its purpose is to teach men the secret of true freedom. History, then, gives us the concrete examples of the precepts inculcated by Philosophy. The one shows what men should do, the other what men have said and done in the past, and what practical lessons we may draw therefrom for the present day. I would indicate as the third main branch of study, Eloquence, which indeed holds a place of distinction amongst the refined arts. By philosophy we learn the essential truth of things, which by eloquence we so exhibit in orderly adornment as to bring conviction to differing minds. And history provides the light of experience—a cumulative wisdom fit to supplement the force of reason and the persuasion of eloquence. For we allow that soundness of judgment, wisdom of speech, integrity of conduct are the marks of a truly liberal temper.

We are told that the Greeks devised for their sons a course of training in four subjects: letters, gymnastics, music, and drawing. Now, of these drawing has no place among our liberal studies; except insofar as it is identical with writing (which is in reality one side of the art of drawing), it belongs to the painter's profession: the Greeks, as an art-loving people, attached to it an exceptional value.

The art of Letters, however, rests upon a different footing. It is a study adapted to all times and to all circumstances, to the investigation of fresh knowledge or to the recasting and application of old. Hence the importance of grammar and of the rules of composition must be recognized at the outset, as the foundation on which the whole study of Literature must rest: and closely associated with these rudiments, the art of Disputation or logical argument. The function of this is to enable us to discern fallacy from truth in discussion. Logic, indeed, as setting forth the true method of learning, is the guide to the acquisition of knowledge in whatever subject. Rhetoric comes next, and is strictly speaking the formal study by which we attain the art of Eloquence; which, as we have just stated, takes the third place among the studies specially important in public life. It is now, indeed, fallen from its old renown and is well-nigh a lost art. In the Law court, in the Council, in the popular Assembly, in exposition, in persuasion, in debate, eloquence finds no place nowadays: speed, brevity, homeliness are the only qualities desired. Oratory, in which our forefathers gained so great glory for themselves and for their language, is despised: but our youth, if they would earn the repute of true education, must emulate their ancestors in this accomplishment.

After Eloquence we place Poetry and the Poetic Art, which though not without their value in daily life and as an aid to oratory, have nevertheless their main concern for the leisure side of existence.

As to Music, the Greeks refused the title of "Educated" to anyone who could not sing or play. Socrates set an example to the Athenian youth, by himself learning to play in his old age; urging the pursuit of music not as a sensuous indulgence, but as an aid to the inner harmony of the soul. Insofar as it is taught as a healthy recreation for the moral and spiritual nature, Music is a truly liberal art, and, both as regards its theory and its practice, should find a place in education.

Arithmetic, which treats of the properties of numbers, Geometry, which treats of the properties of dimensions, lines, surfaces, and solid bodies, are weighty studies because they possess a peculiar element of certainty. The science of the stars, their motions, magnitudes, and distances, lifts us into the clear calm of the upper air. There we may contemplate the fixed stars, or the conjunctions of the planets, and predict the eclipses of the sun and the moon. The knowledge of Nature—animate and inanimate—the laws and the properties of things in heaven and in earth, their causes, mutations, and effects—especially the explanation of their wonders (as they are popularly supposed) by the unraveling of their causes—this is a most delightful, and at the same time most profitable, study for youth. With these may be joined investigations concerning the weights of bodies, and those relative to the subject which mathematicians call "Perspective."

I may here glance for a moment at the three great professional disciplines: Medicine, Law, Theology. Medicine, which is applied science, has undoubtedly much that makes it attractive to a student. But it cannot be described as a liberal study. Law, which is based upon moral philosophy, is undoubtedly held in high respect. Regarding Law as a subject of study, such respect is entirely deserved: but Law as practiced becomes a mere trade. Theology, on the other hand, treats of themes removed from our senses, and attainable only by pure intelligence.

4. The principal "Disciplines" have now been reviewed. It must not be supposed that a liberal education requires acquaintance with them all: for a thorough mastery of even one of them might fairly be the achievement of a lifetime. Most of us, too, must learn to be content with modest capacity as with modest fortune. Perhaps we do wisely to pursue that study which we find most suited to our intelligence and our tastes, though it is true that we cannot rightly understand one subject unless we can perceive its relation to the rest. The choice of studies will depend to some extent upon the

character of individual minds. For while one boy seizes rapidly the point of which he is in search and states it ably, another, working far more slowly, has yet the sounder judgment and so detects the weak spot in his rival's conclusions. The former, perhaps, will succeed in poetry, or in the abstract sciences; the latter in real studies and practical pursuits. Or a boy may be apt in thinking, but slow in expressing himself; to him the study of Rhetoric and Logic will be of much value. Where the power of talk alone is remarkable I hardly know what advice to give. Some minds are strong on the side of memory: these should be apt for history. But it is of importance to remember that in comparison with intelligence memory is of little worth, though intelligence without memory is, so far as education is concerned, of none at all. For we are not able to give evidence that we know a thing unless we can reproduce it.

Again, some minds have peculiar power in dealing with abstract truths, but are defective on the side of the particular and the concrete, and so make good progress in mathematics and in metaphysic. Those of just opposite temper are apt in Natural Science and in practical affairs. And the natural bent should be recognized and followed in education. Let the boy of limited capacity work only at that subject in which he shows he can attain some result.

Respecting the general place of liberal studies, we remember that Aristotle would not have them absorb the entire interests of life: for he kept steadily in view the nature of man as a citizen, an active member of the State. For the man who has surrendered himself absolutely to the attractions of Letters or of speculative thought follows, perhaps, a self-regarding end and is useless as a citizen or as prince. . . .

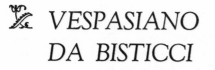

VESPASIANO
DA BISTICCI

Born near Florence in 1421, Vespasiano became perhaps the most famous dealer in manuscripts and books of the entire Renaissance period. A dedicated bibliophile as well as a successful businessman, he enjoyed the personal friendship of many of his distinguished clients, including Cosimo de' Medici, virtual though unofficial ruler of Florence for nearly thirty years, the noted humanist Nicolò Nicoli, and Federigo of Montefeltro, who as Duke of Urbino was celebrated as a great military leader and patron of learning and the arts. Vespasiano's bookshop in Florence served throughout the 1460s and '70s as an informal meeting place for learned men, and it was there that he formed many of the impressions that make his *Vite di uomini illustri del Secolo XV* (*Lives of Illustrious Men of the Fifteenth Century*) such a vivid, engrossing document.

The *Lives* is comprised of 106 brief biographies of important Europeans (almost all Italians) of the fifteenth century—Popes, prelates, rulers, statesmen, and writers. Like many other Florentines of his time, Vespasiano was firmly convinced that his own time represented a golden age for all the arts, following upon centuries of cultural darkness. He held that the great awakening had begun with Dante, continued in Petrarch, Boccaccio, and Salutati, and reached its height under the Medici. He also thought that men's achievements would cease to be remembered and would eventually disappear if they were not set down in writing. This, at least, is his explanation for the *Lives*. Here he was influenced by the Roman biographical tradition revived with great enthusiasm by the humanists, who bowed to none in their concern for fame and honor in the eyes of future generations. As Vespasiano might well have hoped, his accounts of other men's lives have served to establish and assure his own renown.

The following selection presents the lives of two of the most interesting and important contributors to the humanistic culture of the Renaissance, Poggio Bracciolini and Nicolò Nicoli. They provide brief but telling descriptions of these men and their works, and give some useful glimpses of their personal and social milieu. It should be noted that although these men are cultural heroes to Vespasiano, he does not hesitate to present the more negative aspects of their characters in his balanced accounts. (From *The Vespasiano Memoirs*, by Vespasiano da Bisticci. London: Routledge & Kegan Paul, Ltd., 1926, pp. 351-57, 395-403. Recently reprinted as *Renaissance Princes, Popes, and Prelates: The Vespasiano Memoirs: Lives of Illustrious Men of the XVth Century*. New York: Harper & Row, Publishers [Harper Torchbook] 1963. Reprinted by permission of Routledge & Kegan Paul, Ltd.)

From Vespasiano's *Lives*

POGGIO FIORENTINO (1380-1454)

Messer Poggio was born at Terranuova, a Florentine village. His father sent him to the University, where he remained as a teacher, being very learned in the Latin tongue and well conversant with Greek. He was an excellent scribe in ancient characters, and in his youth he was wont to write for a living, providing himself thus with money for the purchase of books and for his other needs. It is well known that the court of Rome is a place where distinguished men may find a position and reward for their activity, and thither he accordingly went, and when his quickness of wit had become known, he was appointed apostolic secretary. Afterward he opened a scrivener's [notary's] office, and in these two vocations was known as a man of integrity and good repute. He had no mind to enter the priesthood, or to accept ecclesiastical preferment, but he took as wife a lady of the noblest blood of Florence, one of the Buondelmonti, and by her had four sons and one daughter. He was sent by Pope Martin with letters into England, and he found much to censure in the way of life of that country, how the people were fain to spend all their time in eating and drinking; indeed, by way of joke, he would tell how, when he had been invited by some bishop or nobleman to dine or sup, he had been forced, after sitting four hours at table, to rise and bathe his eyes with cold water to prevent him[self] from falling asleep. He had many marvelous tales to tell about the wealth of the land. . . .

It was said that his gold and silver plate was of enormous value, and that all the kitchen utensils were of silver, as were also the and-irons and all the smaller articles. Another fellow citizen of ours, Antonio dei Pazzi, went thither also, and one morning, on a solemn feast, the cardinal assembled a great company for which two rooms were prepared, hung with the richest cloth and arranged all round to hold silver ornaments, one of them being full of cups of silver, and the other with cups gilded or golden. Afterward Pazzi was taken into a very sumptuous chamber, and seven strong boxes full of English articles of price were exhibited to him. . . .

When the Council of Constance was assembled, Poggio went thither, and was besought by Nicolò [Nicoli] and other learned men not to spare himself trouble in searching through the religious houses in these parts for some of the many Latin books which had been lost. He found six Orations of Cicero, and, as I understood him to say, found them in a heap of waste paper among the rubbish. He found the complete works of Quintilian, which had hitherto been only known in fragments, and as he could not obtain the volume he spent thirty-two days in copying it with his own hand: this I saw in the fairest manuscript. Every day he filled a copybook with the text. He found Tully's [Cicero's] *De Oratore,* which had been long lost and was known only in parts, Silius Italicus, *De secundo bello punico* [*The Second Punic War*], in heroic verse, Marcus Manilius on Astronomy, written in verse, and the poem of Lucretius, *De rerum Natura* [*Concerning the Nature of Things*], all works of the highest importance. . . .

Next at Constance he found Tully's letters to Atticus, but of these I have no information, and Messer Leonardo [Bruni] and Messer Poggio together discovered the last twelve comedies of Plautus, which Gregorio Corero, Poggio, and certain others amended and set in the order which they still follow. The Verrine orations of Cicero also came from Constance and were brought to Italy by Leonardo and Poggio. Thus it may be seen how many noble works we possess through the efforts of these scholars, and how much we are indebted to them; and how greatly the students of our own time have been enlightened by their discoveries. There was no copy of Pliny in Italy; but, news having been brought to Nicolò that there was a fine and perfect one at Lübeck in Germany, he worked so effectively through Cosimo de' Medici that he, by the agency of a kinsman of his living there, bargained with the friars who owned it, giving them a hundred Rhenish ducats in exchange for the book. But great trouble followed, both to the friars and to the purchasers.

After his return from Constance Poggio commenced [to be an] author, and to show his quality as a speaker. He had a great gift of words, as the study of his writings and translations will show. His letters are most delightful from their easy style, written without effort. He was given to strong invective, and all stood in dread of him. He was a very cultured and pleasant man, sincere and liberal, and the foe of all deceit and pretense. He had many witty stories to tell of adventures he had encountered in England and Germany when he went thither. As he was very free of speech he incurred the ill will of some of their learned men, and was prompt to take up his pen in vituperation of certain men of letters. He wrote a very abusive letter to Pope Felix, the Duke of Savoy, and took up the cudgels in defense of Nicolò Nicoli, on the score of his many virtues, against a learned man who is now dead. Nicolò was devoted to Carlo d'Arezzo [a humanist and academician] on account of his learning and of his excellent character, and procured advancement for him in many ways. By his influence Carlo was appointed to teach in the University in competition with the learned man before named, against whom Poggio, from his love of Nicolò Nicoli, had written his invective. The gathering at Messer Carlo's lectures was marvelous; thither came all the court of Rome, which was then at Florence, and all the learned Florentines, and from this cause arose the differences between Nicolò Nicoli and Filelfo [poet and humanist], through the great reputation which Messer Carlo had thereby gained. Poggio defended Nicolò Nicoli against an attack made by Filelfo, and on this account ill-feeling arose between Nicolò and Filelfo. As much abuse passed from one to the other, and as Cosimo de' Medici was well disposed to Nicolò and Messer Carlo, Filelfo began to trouble the state, and for his misdemeanor was banished as a rebel; so high did feeling run. To return to Messer Poggio. His fame increased all over the world wherever his works were known, and he spent in original writing or in translating all the time he had to spare after attending to his secretarial and his scrivener's office. . . .

While he tarried at Rome, enjoying the highest favor of the Pope, Messer Carlo d' Arezzo, the Chancellor of the Signoria, died at Florence and Poggio was elected to the office forthwith on account of his fame, and his appointment met with general approval. When this news was brought to him, although from his high position at the court of Rome, and the profit he made, he could not hope to better his condition, he felt a desire to return to his country, so he accepted the office and made Florence his fatherland, as it was just to do. Coming from the court of Rome, and being of a disposition open and frank, and without any leaning toward falsity or dissimulation, Poggio by his character was unacceptable to many of those who ruled their conduct by opposite maxims, saying one thing and meaning another.

It happened that an election was held and that he was put forward as a candidate, wherefore he sent word through one of his friends to the electors, who gave him favorable promises as to what they would do. Messer Poggio, who knew little of the Florentine character, took all this for truth, having yet much to learn; and after he had come to an understanding with his friend, and after the ballot boxes had been emptied, he found that he had received nothing but white beans [blackballs]. Deceit was foreign to Poggio, and up to this time he had believed that what so many citizens had said must have been near the truth; but when he saw that he had been tricked, he lost patience at the duplicity of the Florentines, and broke the peace with them, saying that he could never have believed that men would have trangressed into such evil ways, and lamenting that he had come to live in Florence. He believed that this false trick had been played on himself, and not on his friend.

After he had lived some time in Florence he was chosen into the Signoria in order to honor him with [a position of] civic dignity. When he ceased to attend the Signoria—still retaining the chancellorship and discharging his duties—he went to the Roman court, having won approval from the papal authorities by his letters from all parts of the world. Then it was that certain Florentines, of the sort which is always ready to find fault with everything, began to censure him, scheming how, by the agency of Cosimo de' Medici, who was well disposed toward him, they might drive him out of the chancellorship and put another in his place. Let everyone mark what great danger a man incurs who, with many competitors, submits to the popular vote. Messer Poggio, who was growing old, perceived he could not satisfy this demand because it was mixed up with various parties and policies, [and] decided to retire, in order to have more rest. and leisure for study, and let them put another in his office.

Life in the city was uncongenial to his habits and pursuits. Cosimo was much attached to him, and would never have wished to see anyone else in the chancellorship, but when he saw that Messer Poggio cared naught in the matter, he let things take their course, otherwise he would not have allowed the change. Messer Poggio was at this time very rich through long residence at the court of Rome. He had much ready money, property, many houses in Florence, fine household goods, and a noble library: wherefore there was no reason why he should save. Having done with the Palazzo, and with time on his hands, he began upon the history of Florence, taking up the work where Messer Leonardo [Bruni] had left it, and bringing it down to his own day. In Florence it was considered a work of great merit. It had been agreed that he should pay to the state a certain annual sum so that neither he nor his children in the future should be subject to the public burdens of Florence. It came to pass that this privilege was abrogated by an additional tax which laid upon him the insupportable levy of two hundred florins. Hearing the same, Messer Poggio lost patience that the exemption granted to him should be broken in his own lifetime, and if it had not been that Cosimo, who had great influence with him, was able to moderate his anger, he might have

taken some imprudent action, for he could not see that a return
like this was the meet reward for all his labor. The city itself, and
all those who had the Latin tongue, were under great obligations
to him, to Messer Leonardo, and Fra Ambrogio [Traversari (1386-
1431), humanist and theologian], the first exponents of Latin, which
had lain obscure and neglected for so many centuries. Thus Florence found itself, in this golden age, full of learned men.

Among the other exceptional debts which the city of Florence
owed to Messer Leonardo and to Messer Poggio may be reckoned
the following: From the times of the Roman republic onward there
was not to be found any republic or popular state in Italy so
famous as was the city of Florence, which had its history written by
two authors so illustrious as were Messer Leonardo and Messer
Poggio; indeed, before they wrote all knowledge of the same lay in
the deepest obscurity. If the chronicles of the Venetian republic,
with its numerous men of learning, which has wrought such great
deeds both by land and sea, had been written down and not left
unrecorded, the renown of Venice would stand higher than it stands
today. . . . Every republic ought to set high value upon its writers
who may record what is done therein; as we may see from what
has been done in Florence, in a narrative from the very beginning
of the state, to the times of Messer Leonardo and Messer Poggio;
every deed done by the Florentines being set down in Latin in a
narrative appropriate to the same. Poggio let his history follow that
of Leonardo, writing also in Latin, and Giovanni Villani wrote a
general history in the vulgar tongue, telling of what happened in
every place, mixing with it the history of Florence, and following
him Filippo Villani did the same. These two [the Villanis, early
Florentine chroniclers] are the only historians who exhibit these
times to us in their writings.

Anyone who may have to write the Life of Messer Poggio will
find many things to tell, but having had to make something by
way of a commentary, this, which is written here of him, is enough
for the present. . . . Before he died, having left to his children
a good income as it has been already noticed, he made plans for
a marble tomb in S. Croce and stated his wishes as to the erection
of the same, writing the epitaph with his own hand, but afterward,

while the affair was in progress, the money was put to bad use and the tomb was never built. . . .

NICOLÒ NICOLI (*d. 1437*)

Nicolò was well born, one of the four sons of a rich merchant, all of whom became merchants. In his youth Nicolò, by his father's wish, entered trade, wherefore he could not give his time to letters as he desired. After his father's death he left his brothers so as to carry out his aims. He was the master of a good fortune and took up Latin letters, in which he soon became proficient. He studied under [Manuel] Chrysoloras, a learned Greek who had recently come to Florence, and although he worked hard in Greek and Latin he was not content with his progress, so he went to study with Luigi Marsigli [d. 1394; Florentine humanist and political writer], a learned philosopher and theologian, and in the course of some years' reading gained a good knowledge of the subjects he studied. He here acted like a good and faithful Christian, for, putting all else aside, he studied theology alone. Nicolò may justly be called the father and the benefactor of all students of letters, for he gave them protection and encouragement to work, and pointed out to them the rewards which would follow. If he knew of any Greek or Latin book which was not in Florence he spared neither trouble nor cost until he should procure it; indeed, there are numberless Latin books which the city possesses through his care. He gained such high reputation amongst men of letters that Messer Leonardo sent him his *Life of Cicero* and pronounced him to be the censor [i.e., foremost critic] of the Latin tongue.

He was a man of upright life who favored virtue and censured vice. He collected a fine library, not regarding the cost, and was always searching for rare books. He bought all these with the wealth which his father had left, putting aside only what was necessary for his maintenance. He sold several of his farms and spent the proceeds on his library. He was a devoted Christian, who specially favored monks and friars, and was the foe of evildoers. He held his books rather for the use of others than of himself, and all lettered students of Greek or Latin would come to him to borrow books, which he would always lend. He was guileless and sincere and liberal to everyone. It was through his good offices that Fra Ambrogio and Carlo d'Arezzo achieved success, on account of his gifts, the loan of his books, and the fees he paid to their teachers. If he heard of students going to Greece or to France or elsewhere he would give them the names of books which they lacked in Florence, and procure for them the help of Cosimo de' Medici who would do anything for him. When it happened that he could only get the copy of a book he would copy it himself, either in current or shaped characters, all in the finest script, as may be seen in San Marco, where there are many books from his hand in one lettering or the other. He procured at his own expense the works of Tertullian and other [ancient] writers which were not in Italy. He also found an imperfect copy of Ammianus Marcellinus and wrote it out with his own hand. The *De Oratore* and the *Brutus* [by Cicero] were sent to Nicolò from Lombardy, having been brought by the envoys of Duke Filippo when they went to ask for peace in the time of Pope Martin. The book was found in a chest in a very old church; this chest had not been opened for a long time, and they found the book, a very ancient example, while searching for evidence concerning certain ancient rights. *De Oratore* was found broken up, and it is through the care of Nicolò that we find it perfect today. He also rediscovered many sacred works and several of Tully's orations.

Through Nicolò Florence acquired many fine works of sculpture, of which he had great knowledge as well as of painting. A complete copy of Pliny did not exist in Florence, but when Nicolò heard that there was one in Lübeck, in Germany, he secured it by Cosimo's aid, and thus Pliny came to Florence. All the young men he knew in Florence used to come to him for instruction in letters, and he cared for the needs of all those who wanted books or teachers. He did not seek any office in Florence, [although] he was made an official in the University; many times he was selected for some governorship, but he refused them all, saying that they were food for the vultures, and he would let these feed on them. He called vultures those who went into the alehouses and devoured the poor. Master Paolo and Ser Filippo were his intimate friends, and there were few days when they would not be found at the monastery of the Agnoli, together with Fra Ambrogio and sometimes Cosimo and Lorenzo de' Medici, who, on account of Nicolò's great merits, treated him most liberally, because he had spent in books almost all that he had. His means only allowed him to live very sparingly considering his position. The Medici, as they knew this, gave orders at the bank that whenever Nicolò might ask for money, it should be given to him, and charged to their account. They afterward told Nicolò not to let himself want for anything, but to send to the bank for whatever he needed. So Nicolò, being in sore straits, heartened himself to do what he would not otherwise have done. They supported him in this way till the end of his life, and they showed the greatest courtesy in aiding him in necessity. In 1420 Cosimo fled from the plague to Verona, taking with him Nicolò and Carlo d' Arezzo and paying all their charges. Afterward, when Cosimo was banished to Venice, Nicolò was deeply grieved on account of the love he had for him, and one day he wrote a letter to Cosimo at Venice, and when he gave it to the horseman who would deliver it, he said in my presence: "Give this letter to Cosimo, and tell him, Nicolò says that so many ill-deeds are committed by the state every day, that a ream of paper would not suffice him to write them down." And he spoke these words in so loud a voice that all those present could hear them. . . .

His was a frank and liberal nature. One day when he was in company with a friar who was learned rather than pious, he addressed him, saying: "There will be few of your kind in Paradise." Another friar, Francesco da Pietropane by name, lived with a few others in the mountains near Lucca, in pious community, and was a man well versed in Greek and Latin. Nicolò showed them much favor and let them have all the books they wanted. At his death he had lent here and there more than two hundred volumes, among which were some of the Greek books which had been lent to Fra Francesco. This friar, amongst many other gifts, had that of predicting the future, and before Cosimo was banished he informed Nicolò that the year 1433 would bring great danger to Cosimo; he would either lose his life or be exiled, whereupon Nicolò sent word to Cosimo to be on his guard, for in this same year he would be in peril either of death or exile. Cosimo was loath to believe this, but these words proved true. Nicolò had a pure mind, and his conversation was that of a good and faithful Christian, for he would say that there were many unbelievers and rebels against the Christian religion who argued against the immortality of the soul, as if this were a matter of doubt. That it was a great misfortune to many that they were only able to care for their bodies, thinking of their souls, which are no way concerned with their unbridled lusts, as something which could sit in a chair, as something substantial enough to be seen with the eye. All those who were not good Christians and doubted concerning that religion to which he was so firmly attached, incurred his strongest hatred; indeed, it seemed to him stark madness to have any doubt of anything so noble which had won the support of so many wonderful men in every age.

Beyond his other remarkable qualities he had a wide judgment, not only in letters, but also in painting and in sculpture, and he had in his house a number of medals, in bronze, silver, and gold; also many antique figures in copper, and heads in marble. One day, when Nicolò was leaving his house, he saw a boy who had around his neck a chalcedony engraved with a figure by the hand of Polycleitus, a beautiful work. He enquired of the boy his father's name, and having learned this, sent to ask him if he would sell the stone; the father readily consented, like one who neither knew what it was nor valued it. Nicolò sent him five florins in exchange, and the good man to whom it had belonged deemed that he had paid him more than double its value. Nicolò afterward exhibited it as a remarkable object, as indeed it was. There was in Florence in the time of Pope Eugenius a certain Maestro Luigi, the Patriarch, who took great interest in such things as these, and he sent word to Nicolò, asking if he might see the chalcedony. Nicolò sent it to him, and it pleased him so greatly that he kept it, and sent to Nicolò two hundred golden ducats and he urged him so much that Nicolò, not being a rich man, let him have it. After the death of this Patriarch it passed to Pope Paul, and then to Lorenzo de' Medici.

Nicolò had a great knowledge of all parts of the world, so that if anyone who had been in any particular region, and asked him about it, Nicolò would know it better than the man who had been there, and he gave many instances of this. Nicolò always had his house full of distinguished men, and the leading youths of the city. As to the strangers who visited Florence at that time, they all deemed that if they had not visited Nicolò they had not been to Florence at all. Many prelates and learned youths and courtiers frequented his house, and among those who often went to see him was Messer Gregorio Correro, nephew of the Cardinal of Bologna, who himself was the nephew of Pope Gregory. This Messer Gregorio was a mirror of conduct, well read in prose and in verse, and much devoted to Nicolò. As soon as Gregorio, or any other of these youths, should come to him, he put a book into his hand, and bade him read it. There would often be, at the same time, ten or twelve noble young gentlemen with books in their hands reading; after a time he would bid them put down the books and tell him what they had been studying. Then there would be a discussion on some matter of interest so that no time might be lost. Indeed, with Nicolò the custom was absolutely different from that of other houses, where men would sit down to play or gamble at once. It chanced one day that a scholar brought some of his writings to show to him, but neither the subject nor the style of them was to Nicolò's liking. After he had read separate portions of the work, the writer begged for his opinion, but Nicolò demurred, being unwilling to vex him, and answered, "I have already to deal with several hundred volumes of authors of repute before I shall be able to consider yours" (for every writer of that time would ask him to read his work and give an opinion), and handed the manuscript back to the writer, who was much astonished, and failed to understand what his verdict was. He was very apt at composition, but his taste was so delicate that he could rarely satisfy himself. I have spoken formerly with some who have seen his Latin epistles and other elegant writings, but these were not shown to me for reasons which I fully understood.

Nicolò always encouraged promising students to follow a literary life, and he nobly aided all those who showed merit in providing them with teachers and books, for in his time teachers and books were not so numerous as they are today. It may be said that he was the reviver of Greek and Latin letters in Florence; they had for a long time lain buried, and although Petrarch, Dante, and Boccaccio had done something to rehabilitate them, they had not reached that height which they attained through Nicolò's cultivation of them for diverse reasons. First, because he urged many in his time to take to letters, and, through his persuasion, many scholars came to Florence for study and teaching; for instance, he and Palla Strozzi induced Manuel Chrysoloras to come by providing money for his journey. He did the same for Aurispa [another celebrated Greek scholar] and other learned men, and when the question arose of spending money he would say to certain of those he knew, "I wish you would help bring over Manuel, or someone else," and then he would say what each one might give.

Nicolò patronized painters, sculptors, and architects as well as men of letters, and he had a thorough knowledge of their crafts. . . . He was a true connoisseur of all fine things. Friar Ambrogio, Messer Poggio, and Carlo d'Arezzo were his friends, and it was through him that these men of genius became public teachers in Florence in the time of Pope Eugenius. He was on terms of friendship with all the learned men of Italy, and he corresponded with them both at home and abroad.

After having done so many good deeds, and gathered together a vast number of books on all the liberal arts in Greek and Latin, he desired that these should be made accessible to everyone. He directed that, after his death, they should continue to be at the service of all, so in his will be designated forty citizens to see that the books in question should be made a public library in order that all might use them. There were eight hundred volumes of Greek and Latin. He gave directions to these forty citizens that these books should be given to Cosimo de' Medici for the library of San Marco, in fulfillment of the wishes of the testator, that they should remain in a public place for the use of those who might want to consult them. Also that it should be written in the cover of every book how it had once belonged to Nicolò Nicoli, and thus they remain to the present day. The value of them was six thousand florins. At the end of his book, *De longaevis,* Messer Giannozzo [Manetti (1396-1459)] mentions Nicolò and his way of life and the high praise he earned. Among other things he praises most highly the gift of this library, and says that he did more than Plato, Aristotle, or Theophrastus had done, for in the last testaments of Plato and Aristotle are named certain goods which they left to their children, and to others, but they made no mention of their books. Theophrastus left all his possessions privately to a friend; Nicolò alone dedicated his to the public use, therefore much gratitude is due to him. Nor was this all, for Giovanni Boccaccio at his death had left all his books to Santo Spirito, where they were kept in chests, but Nicolò decided that they ought rather to be in a library available for all, so at his own expense he built one for their reception and preservation, and for the honor of Messer Giovanni. As they were for public use he made shelves for them, and they may be seen there to the present time.

To describe Nicolò, he was of handsome presence, lively, with a smile usually on his face, and pleasant manner in conversation. His clothes were always of fine red cloth down to the ground; he never took a wife so as not to be hindered in his studies. He had a housekeeper to provide for his wants, and was one of the most particular of men in his diet as in all else, and was accustomed to have his meals served to him in beautiful old dishes; his table would be covered with vases of porcelain, and he drank from a cup of crystal or of some other fine stone. It was a pleasure to see him at table, old as he was. All the linen that he used was of the whitest. Some may be astonished to hear that he possessed a vast number of vessels, and to these may be answered that, in his day, things of this sort were not so highly prized as now; but Nicolò, being known all over the world, those who wished to please him would send him either marble statues, or antique vases, or sculpture, or marble inscriptions, or pictures by distinguished masters, or tables in mosaic. He had a fine map of the world on which all places were given, and also illustrations of Italy and Spain. There was no house in Florence better decorated than his or better furnished with beautiful things. Nicolò was now over sixty-five years of age; his life had been occupied with good deeds, and when sickness came he was fain to show how his death might be worthy of his life. He was aware that he was near his end, so he sent for Friar Ambrogio and several other holy men and begged them to stay by him till the end. He was a great friend of Maestro Paolo, who, besides being a physician, was a man of holy life, and he begged him to remain also. As he could not rise from his bed he bade them prepare an altar in his room, and all things necessary for the mass; he also made full confession, and then begged Friar Ambrogio to say mass there every morning. After the mass an epistle of Saint Paul, for whom he had the greatest reverence, would be read, and during the reading, when the friar came to any fine passage, he would beg him to stop and would reflect over what had been read, and according to Friar Ambrogio he rarely heard one of these fine passages without tears. He also told me that his fervor and his devotion were wonderful, the result of a well-spent life. He knew that his conscience was clear; that he had never deprived anyone of wealth or fame, and that he had never desired any office in which he might have to pass sentence on others. His room was always filled with those who were the servants of God; unbelievers kept away, knowing that he did not care for them.

At the end he did his religious duties with great devotion. First mass was said, then he had himself placed on the ground on a carpet, with a large number of persons kneeling around him. When the Host was presented he showed the greatest devotion, and he turned to his Redeemer and accused himself as a sinner, and as one unworthy of this holy sacrament. Those around him could scarcely restrain their tears. This wonderful grace came from his habit of always reading holy books. Having taken the sacred body of Christ from the hands of Friar Ambrogio he seemed greatly consoled, and would only speak of his own salvation or read some book of devotion or discourse with the holy men about him. These were the exercises of his last illness, and when his end came he died in the arms of Friar Ambrogio, like a holy man who from his childhood had lived a godly life.

✒ LORENZO VALLA

Valla is probably the most famous humanist of the fifteenth century, and was almost certainly the most influential. Erasmus described Valla as "a man who with so much energy, zeal, and labor, refuted the stupidities of the barbarians, saved half-buried letters from extinction, restored Italy to her ancient splendor of eloquence, and forced even the learned to express themselves henceforth with more circumspection." Valla left few areas of humanistic studies untouched. As a Biblical scholar, he made important attempts to apply humanistic philological methods to Scriptural texts. As a philosopher, he wrote on pleasure, dialectic, and the freedom of the will. As a stylist, he provided a Latin handbook used by students for centuries. As a controversialist, his invectives were directed against various people, and his pen was feared. As a translator, he made Herodotus and Thucydides available in Latin. As a historian, he recounted the reign of King Ferdinand I of Aragon, and wrote the treatise from which the present selection comes.

A Roman by birth and education, he became a professor of eloquence at the University of Pavia in 1429. He remained there until 1433, when he had to flee because of the furor aroused against him by his vitriolic attack on the legal theories of the celebrated jurist Bartolus of Sassoferato (1314-1357) and his school. In 1437 he became secretary to King Alfonso of Aragon, who retained Valla at his court in Naples until 1448. In that year he returned to Rome. Until his death in 1457 at the age of fifty, he served as a papal secretary, and as professor at the university.

The treatise on the Donation of Constantine was written in 1440, while Valla was in King Alfonso's service. When Valla wrote, the Donation was regarded as a grant by the

55

Emperor Constantine to the Papacy, in gratitude for his conversion by Pope Sylvester, both of spiritual supremacy and of temporal rule of Rome, of Italy, and of the entire western part of the Roman Empire for all time. In this major attempt to apply philological techniques to the analysis of the document upon which the territorial claims of the papacy rested, Valla proved the Donation a forgery. (We now know that it was forged at Rome in the last half of the eighth century.) The present excerpts include the introductory pages of Valla's treatise, and some of the historical arguments from the concluding section. The philological parts, which are fascinating, have been omitted from this text because they are too technical to be understood from a brief excerpt. Valla's polemical tone is natural to him, but it also reflects the fact that he writes in the service of a king who wishes to discredit the secular claims of the Church. (From *The Treatise of Lorenzo Valla on the Donation of Constantine*, by C. B. Coleman. New Haven, Conn.: Yale University Press, 1922, pp. 21-29, 163-83. Reprinted by permission of Yale University Press.)

The Discourse of Lorenzo Valla on the Forgery of the Alleged Donation of Constantine

I have published many books, a great many, in almost every branch of learning. Inasmuch as there are those who are shocked that in these I disagree with certain great writers already approved by long usage, and charge me with rashness and sacrilege, what must we suppose some of them will do now! How they will rage against me, and if opportunity is afforded how eagerly and how quickly they will drag me to punishment! For I am writing against not only the dead, but the living also, not this man or that, but a host, not merely private individuals, but the authorities. And what authorities! Even the supreme pontiff, armed not only with the temporal sword as are kings and princes, but with the spiritual also, so that even under the very shield, so to speak, of any prince, you cannot protect yourself from him; from being struck down by excommunication, anathema, curse. So if he was thought to have both spoken and acted prudently who said, "I will not write against those who can write 'Proscribed,'" how much more would it seem that I ought to follow the same course toward him who goes far beyond proscription, who would pursue me with the invisible darts of his authority, so that I could rightly say, "Whither shall I go from thy spirit, or whither shall I flee from thy presence?" Unless perhaps we think the supreme pontiff would bear these attacks more patiently than would others. Far from it; for Ananias, the high priest, in the presence of the tribune who sat as judge, ordered Paul, when he said he lived in good conscience, to be smitten on the mouth; and Pashur, holding the same rank, threw Jeremiah into prison for the boldness of his speech. The tribune and the governor, indeed, were able and willing to protect the former, and the king the latter, from priestly violence. But what tribune, what governor, what king, even if he wanted to, could snatch me from the hands of the chief priest if he should seize me?

But there is no reason why this awful, twofold peril should trouble me and turn me from my purpose; for the supreme pontiff may not bind nor loose any one contrary to law and justice. And to give one's life in defense of truth and justice is the path of the highest virtue, the highest honor, the highest reward. Have not many undergone the hazard of death for the defense of their terrestrial fatherland? In the attainment of the celestial fatherland (they attain it who please God, not men), shall I be deterred by the hazard of death? Away then with trepidation, let fears far remove, let doubts pass away. With a brave soul, with utter fidelity, with good hope, the cause of truth must be defended, the cause of justice, the cause of God.

Nor is he to be esteemed a true orator who knows how to speak well, unless he also has the courage to speak. So let us have the courage to accuse him, whoever he is, that commits crimes calling for accusation. And let him who sins against all be called to account by the voice of one speaking for all. Yet perhaps I ought not to reprove my brother in public, but by himself. Rather, "Them that sin" and do not accept private admonition "rebuke before all, that others also may fear." Or did not Paul, whose words I have just used, reprove Peter to his face in the presence of the church because he needed reproof? And he left this written for our instruction. But perhaps I am not a Paul that I should reprove a Peter.

Yea, I am a Paul because I imitate Paul. Just as, and this is far greater, I become one in spirit with God when I diligently observe his commandments. Nor is any one made immune from chiding by an eminence which did not make Peter immune, and many others possessed of the same rank. . . .

It is not my aim to inveigh against any one and write so-called Philippics against him—be that villainy far from me—but to root out error from men's minds, to free them from vices and crimes by either admonition or reproof. I would not dare to say [that my aim is] that others, taught by me, should prune with steel the papal see, which is Christ's vineyard, rank with overabundant shoots, and compel it to bear rich grapes instead of meager wildings. When I do that, is there any one who will want to close either my mouth or his own ears, much less propose punishment and death? If one should do so, even if it were the Pope, what should I call him, a good shepherd, or a deaf viper which would not choose to heed the voice of the charmer, but to strike his limbs with its poisonous bite?

I know that for a long time now men's ears are waiting to hear the offense with which I charge the Roman pontiffs. It is, indeed, an enormous one, due either to supine ignorance, or to gross avarice which is the slave of idols, or to pride of empire of which cruelty is ever the companion. For during some centuries now, either they have not known that the Donation of Constantine is spurious and forged, or else they themselves forged it, and their successors walking in the same way of deceit as their elders have defended as true what they knew to be false, dishonoring the majesty of the pontificate, dishonoring the memory of ancient pontiffs, dishonoring the Christian religion, confounding everything with murders, disasters, and crimes. They say the city of Rome is theirs, theirs the kingdom of Sicily and of Naples, the whole of Italy, the Gauls, the Spains, the Germans, the Britons, indeed the whole West; for all these are contained in the instrument of the Donation itself. So all these are yours, supreme pontiff? And it is your purpose to recover them all? To despoil all kings and princes of the West of their cities or compel them to pay you a yearly tribute, is that your plan?

I, on the contrary, think it fairer to let the princes despoil you of all the empire you hold. For, as I shall show, that Donation whence the supreme pontiffs will have their right derived was unknown equally to Sylvester and to Constantine.

But before I come to the refutation of the instrument of the Donation, which is their one defense, not only false but even stupid, the right order demands that I go further back. And first, I shall show that Constantine and Sylvester were not such men that the former would choose to give, would have the legal right to give, or would have it in his power to give those lands to another, or that the latter would be willing to accept them or could legally have done so. In the second place, if this were not so, though it is absolutely true and obvious, [I shall show that in fact] the latter did not receive nor the former give possession of what is said to have been granted, but that it always remained under the sway and empire of the Caesars. In the third place, [I shall show that] nothing was given to Sylvester by Constantine, but to an earlier Pope (and Constantine had received baptism even before that pontificate), and that the grants were inconsiderable, for the mere subsistence of the Pope. Fourth, that it is not true either that a copy of the Donation is found in the Decretum [of Gratian], or that it was taken from the History of Sylvester; for it is not found in it or in any history, and it is comprised of contradictions, impossibilities, stupidities, barbarisms, and absurdities. Further, I shall speak of the pretended or mock donation of certain other Caesars. Then by way of redundance I shall add that even had Sylvester taken possession, nevertheless, he or some other pontiff having been dispossessed, possession could not be resumed after such a long interval under either divine or human law. Last [I shall show] that the possessions which are now held by the supreme pontiff could not, in any length of time, be validated by prescription [i.e., legal title].

Let[1] us grant that Constantine made the Donation and that Sylvester was at one time in possession, but afterward either he himself or another of the Popes lost possession. (I am speaking now of that of which the Pope is not in possession; later on I will speak of that of which he is in possession.) What more can I grant you than to concede the existence of that which never was and never could be? But even so, I say that you cannot effect a recovery

---

[1] The following passage is taken from the concluding section of the work.

either by divine or by human law. In the ancient law it was forbidden that a Hebrew be a Hebrew's slave more than six years, and every fiftieth year also everything reverted to the original owner. Shall a Christian, in the dispensation of grace, be oppressed in eternal slavery by the vicar of the Christ who redeemed us from our servitude? What do I say! Shall he be recalled to servitude after he has been set free and has long enjoyed his freedom?

How brutal, how violent, how barbarous the tyranny of priests often is, I do not say. If this was not known before, it has lately been learned from that monster of depravity, John Vitelleschi [c.1395-1440; a prelate known mainly for his military exploits], cardinal and patriarch, who wore out the sword of Peter, with which [the apostle] cut off the ear of Malchus, with the blood of Christians. By this sword he himself also perished. But is it true that the people of Israel were permitted to revolt from the house of David and Solomon whom prophets sent by God had anointed, because their impositions were too heavy; and that God approved their act? May we not revolt on account of such great tyranny, particularly from those who are not kings, and cannot be; and who from being shepherds of the sheep, that is to say, of souls, have become thieves and brigands?

And to come to human law, who does not know that there is no right conferred by war, or if there is any, that it prevails just as long as you possess what you have gotten by war? For when you lose possession, you have lost the right. And so ordinarily, if captives have escaped no one summons them into court: and so also with plunder if the former owners have recovered it. Bees and any other kind of winged creatures, if they have flown away far from my property and have settled on another's, cannot be reclaimed. And do you seek to reclaim men, who are not only free creatures, but masters of others, when they set themselves free by force of arms, [reclaim them] not by force of arms, but by law, as though you were a man, and they sheep?

Nor can you say, "The Romans were [considered] just in waging wars against the nations, and just in depriving them of liberty." Do not drag me into that discussion, lest I be forced to speak against my fellow Romans. However, no fault could be so serious that people should merit everlasting servitude therefor. And in this connection [one must remember also] that people often waged a war for which a prince or some important citizen in the Republic was to blame, and, being conquered, were undeservedly punished with servitude. There are everywhere abundant examples of this.

Nor in truth does the law of nature provide that one people should subjugate another people to itself. We can instruct others, we can urge them; we cannot rule them and do them violence, unless, leaving humanity aside, we wish to copy the more savage beasts which force their bloody rule upon the weaker, as the lion among quadrupeds, the eagle among birds, the dolphin among fish. Yet even these creatures do not vaunt authority over their own kind, but over an inferior. How much more ought we to act thus, and as men have due regard for men, since in the words of Marcus Fabius there is no beast upon the earth so fierce that his own likeness is not sacred to him?

Now there are four reasons why wars are waged: either for avenging a wrong and defending friends; or for fear of incurring disaster later, if the strength of others is allowed to increase; or for hope of booty; or for desire of glory. Of these the first is rather honorable, the second less so, and the last two are far from honorable. And wars were indeed often waged against the Romans, but after they had defended themselves, they waged war against their assailants and against others. Nor is there any nation which yielded to their sway unless conquered in war and subdued; whether justly, or for what cause, they themselves could judge. I should be unwilling to condemn them as fighting unjustly or to acquit them as fighting in a just cause. I can only say that the Roman people waged wars against others for the same reason as other peoples and kings did, and that it was left open even to those who were attacked and conquered in war to revolt from the Romans just as they revolted from other masters; lest perchance (and none would agree to this) all authority should be imputed to the oldest people who were first masters; that is, to those who were the first to take possession of what belonged to others.

And yet the Roman people had a better right over nations conquered in war than had the Caesars in their overthrow of the Republic. Wherefore, if it was right for the nations to revolt from Constantine, and, what is far more, from the Roman people, surely it will be right to revolt from him to whom Constantine gave his authority. And to put the matter more boldly, if the Roman people were free either to drive Constantine out, as they did Tarquinius, or to slay him, as they did Julius Caesar, much more will the Romans or the provinces be free to slay him, who at any time has succeeded Constantine. But though this is true, yet it is beyond the scope of my argument, and so I want to restrain myself and not press anything I have said further than this, that it is folly to adduce any verbal right, where the right of arms prevails, because that which is acquired by arms, is likewise lost by arms.

This, indeed, the more, that other, new peoples, as we have heard in the case of the Goths, who were never subject to Roman rule, after putting to flight the earlier inhabitants, seized upon Italy and many provinces. What justice, pray, is there in restoring these to a servitude which they have never experienced; especially as they are the conquering peoples; and to servitude perchance under the conquered peoples? And if at this time any cities and nations, deserted by the Emperor at the arrival of the barbarians, as we know to have been the case, had been compelled to elect a king under whose leadership they then won victory, is there any reason why they should later depose this ruler? Or should they bid his sons, popular it may be for their father's praise, it may be for their own valor, become private citizens, that they might again become subjects of a Roman prince, even though they were greatly in need of their assistance and hoped for no aid elsewhere? If the Caesar himself, or Constantine, returned to life, or even the Senate and Roman people should call them before a general court such as the Amphictyony was in Greece, [the plaintiff] would at once be ruled out at his first plea because he was reclaiming to bondage and slavery those who once had been abandoned by him, their guardian, those who for a long time had been living under another ruler, those who had never been subject to a foreign-born king, men, in conclusion, who were freeborn and proclaimed free by their vigor of mind and body. How clear it should be, that if the Caesar, if the Roman people, is thus debarred from recovering control, much more decidedly is the Pope! And if the other nations which have been subject to Rome are free either to appoint a king for themselves or to maintain a republic, far more are the Roman people themselves free to do this, especially against the innovation of papal tyranny.

Stopped from defending the Donation, since it never existed and, if it had existed, it would now have expired from lapse of time, our adversaries take refuge in another kind of defense; figuratively speaking, the city being given up for lost, they betake themselves to their citadel—which forthwith they are constrained by lack of provisions to surrender. "The Roman church," they say, "is entitled by prescription [i.e., legal title] to what it possesses." Why then does it lay claim to that, the greater part, to which it has no title by prescription, and to which others are entitled by prescription; unless others cannot act toward it as it can act toward them?

The Roman church has title by prescription! Why then does it so often take care to have the Emperors confirm its right? Why does it vaunt the Donation, and its confirmation by the Caesars? If this alone is sufficient, you seriously weaken it by not at the same time keeping silent about the other title [by prescription]. Why don't you keep silent about that other? Obviously because this is not sufficient.

The Roman church has prescribed! And how can it have entered a prescription where no title is established but only possession through bad faith? Or if you deny that the possession was a case of bad faith, at least you cannot deny that the faith [in the Donation] was stupid. Or, in a matter of such importance and notoriety, ought ignorance of fact and of law to be excused? Of fact, because Constantine did not make a grant of Rome and the provinces; a fact of which a man of the common people might well be ignorant, but not the supreme pontiff. Of law, because they could not be granted; which any Christian ought to know. And so, will stupid credulity give you a right to that which, had you been more conscientious, would never have been yours? Well! Now, at least, after I have shown that you held possession through ignorance and stupidity, do you not lose that right, if it was such? and what ignorance unhappily brought you, does not knowledge happily take away again? and does not the property revert from the illegal to the legal master, perchance even with interest? But if you continue to keep possession in the future, your ignorance is henceforth changed into malice aforethought and into deceit, and you become a fraudulent holder.

The Roman church has entered a prescription! O simpletons, O ignoramuses in divine law! No length of years whatever can destroy a true title. Or indeed, if I were captured by barbarians and supposed to have perished, and should return again home after a hundred years of captivity, as a claimant of my paternal inheritance, should I be excluded? What could be more inhuman! And, to give another example, did Jephthah, the leader of Israel, when the Ammonites demanded back the land from "the borders of Arnon even unto Jabbok and unto Jordan," reply, "Israel has prescribed this now through three hundred years' occupation"? Or did he not show that the land which they demanded as theirs, had never been theirs, but had been the Amorites'? And the proof that it did not belong to the Ammonites was that they had never in the course of so many years claimed it.

The Roman church has prescribed! Keep still, impious tongue! You transfer "prescription," which is used of inanimate, senseless objects, to man; and holding man in servitude is the more detestable, the longer it lasts. Birds and wild animals do not let themselves be "prescribed," but however long the time of captivity, when they please and occasion is offered, they escape. And may not man, held captive by man, escape?

Let me tell why the Roman pontiffs show fraud and craft rather than ignorance in using war instead of law as their arbiter—and I believe that the first pontiffs to occupy the city [of Rome] and the other towns did about the same. . . .

Suffice it to say that as often as it could [Rome] has rebelled; as for instance, six years ago, when it could not obtain peace from Eugenius, and it was not equal to the enemies which were besieging it, it besieged the Pope within his house, and would not permit him to go out before he either made peace with the enemy or turned over the administration of the city to the citizens. But he preferred to leave the city in disguise, with a single companion in flight, rather than to gratify the citizens in their just and fair demands. If you give them the choice, who does not know that they would choose liberty rather than slavery?

We may suspect the same of the other cities, which are kept in servitude by the supreme pontiff, though they ought rather to be liberated by him from servitude. It would take too long to enumerate how many cities taken from their enemies the Roman people once set free; it went so far that Titus [Flamininus] set free the whole of Greece, which had been under Antiochus, and directed that it enjoy its own laws. But the Pope, as may be seen, lies in wait assiduously against the liberty of countries; and, therefore, one after another, they daily, as opportunity affords, rebel. (Look at Bologna just now.) And if at any time they have voluntarily accepted papal rule, as may happen when another danger threatens them from elsewhere, it must not be supposed that they have accepted it in order to enslave themselves, so that they could never withdraw their necks from the yoke, so that neither themselves nor those born afterward should have control of their own affairs; for this would be utterly iniquitous.

Of our own will we came to you, supreme pontiff, that you might govern us; of our own will we now leave you again, that you may govern us no more. If you have any claim against us, let the balance of debit and credit be determined. But you want to govern us against our will, as though we were wards of yours, we who perhaps could govern you more wisely than you do yourself! Add to this the wrongs all the time being committed against this state either by you or by your magistrates. We call God to witness that our wrong drives us to revolt, as once Israel did from Rehoboam. And what great wrong did they have? What [a small] part of our calamity is the [mere] payment of heavier taxes! What then if you impoverish the Republic? You *have* impoverished it. What if you despoil our temples? You *have* despoiled them. What if you outrage maidens and matrons? You *have* outraged them. What if you drench the city with the blood of its citizens? You *have* drenched it. Must we endure all this? Nay, rather, since you have ceased to be a father to us, shall we not likewise forget to be sons? This people summoned you, supreme pontiff, to be a father, or if it better pleases you, to be their lord, not to be an enemy and a hangman; you do not choose to act the father or the lord, but the enemy and the hangman. But, since we are Christians, we will not imitate your ferocity and your impiety, even though by the law of reprisal we might do so, nor will we bare the avenging sword above your head; but first your abdication and removal, and then we will adopt another father or lord. Sons may flee from vicious parents who brought them into the world; may we not flee from you, not our real father but an adopted one who treats us in the worst way possible? But

do you attend to your priestly functions; and don't take your stand in
the north, and thundering there hurl your lightning and thunderbolts
against this people and others.

But why need I say more in this case, absolutely self-evident as
it is? I contend that not only did Constantine not grant such great
possessions, not only could the Roman pontiff not hold them by
prescription, but that even if either were a fact, nevertheless either
right would have been extinguished by the crimes of the possessors,
for we know that the slaughter and devastation of all Italy and of
many of the provinces has flowed from this single source. If the
source is bitter, so is the stream; if the root is unclean, so are the
branches; if the first fruit is unholy, so is the lump. And *vice versa,*
if the stream is bitter, the source must be stopped up; if the branches
are unclean, the fault comes from the root; if the lump is unholy,
the first fruit must also be accursed. Can we justify the principle of
papal power when we perceive it to be the cause of such great
crimes and of such great and varied evils?

Wherefore I declare, and cry aloud, nor, trusting God, will I
fear men, that in my time no one in the supreme pontificate has
been either a faithful or a prudent steward, but they have gone so
far from giving food to the household of God that they have devoured it as food and a mere morsel of bread! And the Pope himself makes war on peaceable people, and sows discord among states
and princes. The Pope both thirsts for the goods of others and
drinks up his own: he is what Achilles calls Agamemnon, . . . "a
people-devouring king." The Pope not only enriches himself at the
expense of the republic, as neither Verres nor Catiline nor any
other embezzler dared to do, but he enriches himself at the expense
of even the church and the Holy Spirit as old Simon Magus himself
would abhor doing. And when he is reminded of this and is re-
proved by good people occasionally, he does not deny it, but openly
admits it, and boasts that he is free to wrest from its occupants by
any means whatever the patrimony given the church by Constantine;
as though, when it was recovered, Christianity would be in an ideal
state—and not rather the more oppressed by all kinds of crimes,
extravagances, and lusts; if indeed it can be oppressed more, and
if there is any crime yet uncommitted!

And so, that he may recover the other parts of the Donation, money wickedly stolen from good people he spends more wickedly, and he supports armed forces, mounted and foot, with which all places are plagued, while Christ is dying of hunger and nakedness in so many thousands of paupers. Nor does he know, the unworthy reprobate, that while he works to deprive secular powers of what belongs to them, they in turn are either led by his bad example, or driven by necessity (granting that it may not be a real necessity) to make off with what belongs to the officers of the Church. And so there is no religion anywhere, no sanctity, no fear of God; and, what I shudder to mention, impious men pretend to find in the Pope an excuse for all their crimes. For he and his followers furnish an example of every kind of crime and, with Isaiah and Paul, we can say against the Pope and those about him:

> The name of God is blasphemed among the Gentiles through you, you who teach others, but do not teach yourselves; who preach against stealing and yourselves are robbers; who abhor idols, and commit sacrilege; who make your boast of the law and the pontificate, and through breaking the law dishonor God, the true pontiff.

But if the Roman people through excess of wealth lost the well-known quality of true Romans; if Solomon likewise fell into idolatry through the love of women; should we not recognize that the same thing happens in the case of a supreme pontiff and the other clergy? And should we then think that God would have permitted Sylvester to accept an occasion of sin? I will not suffer this injustice to be done that most holy man, I will not allow this affront to be offered that most excellent pontiff, that he should be said to have accepted empires, kingdoms, provinces, things which those who wish to enter the clergy are wont, indeed, to renounce. Little did Sylvester possess, little also the other holy pontiffs, those men whose presence was inviolable even among enemies, as Leo's presence overawed and broke down the wild soul of the barbarian king, which the strength of Rome had not availed to break down nor overawe. But recent supreme pontiffs, that is, those having riches and pleasures in abundance, seem to work hard to make themselves just as impious and foolish as those early pontiffs were wise and holy, and to extinguish the lofty praises of those men by every possible infamy. Who that calls himself a Christian can calmly bear this?

However, in this my first discourse I do not wish to urge princes and peoples to restrain the Pope in his unbridled course as he roams about, and compel him to stay within bounds, but only to warn him, and perhaps he has already learned the truth, to betake himself from others' houses to his own, and to put to port before the raging billows and savage tempests. But if he refuses, then I will have recourse to another discourse far bolder than this. If only I may sometimes see, and indeed I can scarcely wait to see it, especially if it is brought about by my counsel, if only I may see the time when the Pope is the vicar of Christ alone, and not of Caesar also! If only there would no longer be heard the fearful cry, "Partisans for the Church," "Partisans against the Church," "The Church against the Perugians," "against the Bolognese"! It is not the church, but the Pope, that fights against Christians; the church fights against "spiritual wickedness in high places." Then the Pope will be the Holy Father in fact as well as in name, Father of all, Father of the church; nor will he stir up wars among Christians, but those stirred up by others he, through his apostolic judgment and papal prerogative, will stop.

 POPE PIUS II

Aeneas Sylvius, of the noble Sienese family of the Piccolomini, remains one of the most engaging figures of the Renaissance. Born in 1405, he pursued a varied career as a humanist, courtly secretary to three popes and to Emperor Frederick III, diplomat, and prelate, before his elevation to the papal chair in 1458. Together with nearly universal interests and sympathies —he loved nature, sports, travel, poetry, and the inner workings of diplomacy—he combined an almost boundless self-esteem, and a vanity so frank as to be positively disarming.

Like many another humanist, his youthful writings are of a secular, literary, and historical nature, and include works of history, treatises on education and other subjects, love poetry, extensive correspondence, and elegant orations in Latin. But the work for which the humanist-turned-Pope is best known is his *Commentaries,* in which he recorded the events of his reign as he experienced them. It is one of the most enlightening documents of the period, not only as the expression of a particularly forceful and significant personality, but as a chronicle of the military, political, and diplomatic events of a period of rapid change, as seen by an unusually well informed and articulate observer. It is written in the third person, a fact that for centuries caused considerable confusion as to the identity of the author, until at the end of the nineteenth century the great historian of the papacy, Ludwig von Pastor, discovered conclusive evidence that Pius had written it himself.

The brief excerpts from the *Commentaries* that follow are accounts of the Pope's election, and of his subsequent visit to Florence in 1459. He was on his way to attend a Congress at Mantua that he had called for the purpose of unifying Christendom against the threat of the Turks. With the capture of Constantinople by the Turks in 1453, Pius' project took on new urgency. The passages are characteristic of the *Commentaries* in their curiosity, their attention to observed details and to history, and their dextrous sketches of the people and situations which Pius encountered. The description of Sigismondo Malatesta in the second selection is an exceptionally evocative specimen of the Pope's prose. Sigismondo, it should be noted, is remembered by posterity for the infamous vices of his personal life as well as for the bitter political enmity between himself and the Pope. (From *Memoirs of a Renaissance Pope: The Commentaries of Pius II,* edited by Florence A. Gragg and Leona C. Gabel. New York: G. P. Putnam's Sons, 1959, pp. 79-90, 105-13. Copyright © by Florence A. Gragg and Leona C. Gabel. Reprinted by permission of G. P. Putnam's Sons.)

From Pius II's *Commentaries*

BOOK I

The conclave was held in the apostolic palace at St. Peter's, where two halls and two chapels were set apart for it. In the larger chapel were constructed cells in which the cardinals might eat and sleep; the smaller, called the chapel of San Niccolò, was reserved for discussion and the election of the pope. The halls were places where all might walk about freely.

On the day of their entrance nothing was done about the election. On the next day certain capitulations were announced, which they agreed should be observed by the new pope, and each swore that he would abide by them, should the lot fall on him. On the third day after mass, when they came to the scrutiny, it was found that Filippo, Cardinal of Bologna, and Aeneas [Sylvius], Cardinal of Siena, had an equal number of votes, five apiece. No one else had more than three. On that ballot, whether from strategy or dislike, no one voted for Guillaume, Cardinal of Rouen.

The cardinals were accustomed, after the result of the scrutiny was announced, to sit and talk together in case any wished to change his mind and transfer the vote he had given one to another (a method called "by accession"), for in this way they more easily reach an agreement. This procedure was omitted after the first scrutiny owing to the opposition of those who had received no votes and therefore could not now be candidates for accession. They adjourned for luncheon and then there were many private conferences. The richer and more influential members of the college summoned the rest and sought to gain the papacy for themselves or their friends. They begged, promised, threatened, and some, shamelessly casting aside all decency, pleaded their own causes and claimed the papacy as their right. Among these were Guillaume, Cardinal of Rouen, Pietro, Cardinal of San Marco, and Giovanni, Cardinal of Pavia; nor did the Cardinal of Lerida neglect his own interests. Each had a great deal to say for himself. Their rivalry was extraordinary, their energy unbounded. They took no rest by day or sleep by night.

Rouen, however, did not fear these men so much as he did Aeneas and the Cardinal of Bologna, toward whom he saw the majority of the votes inclining. But he was especially afraid of Aeneas, whose silence he had no doubt would prove far more effective than the barkings of the rest. Therefore he would summon now some, now others, and upbraid them as follows:

> What is Aeneas to you? Why do you think him worthy of the papacy? Will you give us a lame, poverty-stricken pope? How shall a destitute pope restore a destitute church, or an ailing pope an ailing church? He has but recently come from Germany. We do not know him. Perhaps he will even transfer the Curia thither. And look at his writings! Shall we set a poet in Peter's place? Shall we govern the Church by the laws of the heathen? Or do you think Filippo of Bologna is to be preferred? —a stiff-necked fellow, who has not the wit to rule himself, and will not listen to those who show him the right course. I am the senior cardinal. You know I am not without wisdom. I am learned in pontifical law and can boast of royal blood. I am rich in friends and resources with which I can succor the impoverished Church. I hold also not a few ecclesiastical benefices, which I shall distribute among you and the others, when I resign them.

He would then add many entreaties and if they had no effect, he would resort to threats. If anyone brought up his past simony as an indication that in his hands the papacy would be for sale, he did not deny that his past life had been tainted with that stain but swore that in the future his hands should be clean. He was supported by Alain, Cardinal of Avignon, who lent him every assistance in his power, not so much because he was a Frenchman siding with a Frenchman as because, at the elevation of Guillaume, he expected to obtain his house in Rome, the church of Rouen, and the vice-chancellorship. Not a few were won over by Rouen's splendid promises and were caught like flies by their gluttony. And the tunic of Christ without Christ was being sold.

Many cardinals met in the privies as being a secluded and retired place. Here they agreed as to how they might elect Guillaume pope and they bound themselves by written pledges and by oath. Guillaume trusted them and was presently promising benefices and preferment and dividing provinces among them. A fit place for such a pope to be elected! For where could one more appropriately enter into a foul covenant than in privies? Guillaume could certainly count on the two Greeks, the Cardinals of Genoa, San Sisto, Avignon, Colonna, and Pavia. The Vice-Chancellor, the Cardinals of Bologna, Orsini, and Sant' Anastasia were doubtful and seemed likely to accede to him if pushed a little. Indeed they had almost given him definite grounds for hope. Since it now appeared that eleven were agreed, they did not doubt that they would at once get the twelfth. For when it has come to this point, some one is always at hand to say, "I too make you pope," to win the favor that utterance always brings. They thought therefore that the thing was as good as done and were only waiting for daylight to go to the scrutiny.

Some time after midnight the Cardinal of Bologna went hurriedly to Aeneas's cell and waking him said, "Look here, Aeneas! Don't you know that we already have a pope? Some of the cardinals have met in the privies and decided to elect Guillaume. They are only waiting for daylight. I advise you to get up and go and offer him your vote before he is elected, for fear that if he is elected with you against him, he will make trouble for you. I intend to take care not to fall into the old trap. I know what it means to have the pope your enemy. I have had experience with Calixtus, who never gave me a friendly look, because I had not voted for him. It seems to me expedient to curry favor beforehand with the man who is going to be pope. I offer you the advice I am taking myself."

Aeneas answered, "Filippo, away with you and your advice! No one shall persuade me to vote for a man I think utterly unworthy to be the successor of St. Peter. Far from me be such a sin! I will be clean of that crime and my conscience shall not prick me. You say it is hard not to have the pope well-disposed to you. I have no fears on that score. I know he will not murder me because I have not voted for him. 'But,' you say, 'he will not love you, will not make you presents, will not help you. You will feel the pinch of poverty.' Poverty is not hard for one accustomed to it. I have led a life of indigence heretofore; what matter if I die indigent? He will not take from me the Muses, who are all the sweeter in humble fortunes.

"But I am not the man to believe that God will allow the Church, His Bride, to perish in the hands of the Cardinal of Rouen. For what is more alien to the profession of Christ than that His Vicar should be a slave to simony and lewdness? The Divine Mercy will not endure that this palace, which has been the dwelling of so many Holy Fathers, shall become a den of thieves or a brothel of whores. The apostleship is bestowed by God, not by men. Those who have conspired to commit the papacy to Rouen are men; and men's schemes are vain—who does not know it? Well has their conspiracy been made in the privies! Their plots too will have to retire and, like the Arian heresy, their most foul contrivings will end in a most foul place. Tomorrow will show that the Bishop of Rome is chosen by God not by men. As for you, if you are a Christian, you will not choose as Christ's Vicar him whom you know to be a limb of the devil." With these words he frightened Filippo from going over to Rouen.

Next Aeneas went at daybreak to Rodrigo, the Vice-Chancellor, and asked whether he had sold himself to Rouen. "What would you have me do?" he answered, "The thing is settled. Many of the cardinals have met in the privies and decided to elect him. It is not for my advantage to remain with a small minority out of favor with a new pope. I am joining the majority and I have looked out for my own interests. I shall not lose the chancellorship; I have a note from Rouen assuring me of that. If I do not vote for him, the others will elect him anyway and I shall be stripped of my office." Aeneas said to him, "You young fool! Will you then put an enemy of your nation in the Apostle's chair? And will you put faith in the note of a man who is faithless? You will have the note; Avignon will have the chancellorship. For what has been promised you has been promised him also and solemnly affirmed. Will faith be kept with him or with you? Will a Frenchman be more friendly to a Frenchman or to a Catalan? Will he be more concerned for a foreigner or for his own countryman? Take care, you inexperienced boy! Take care, you fool! And if you have no thought for the Church of Rome, if you have no regard for the Christian religion and despise God, for Whom you are preparing such a vicar, at least take thought for yourself, for you will find yourself among the hindmost, if a Frenchman is pope."

The Vice-Chancellor listened patiently to these words of his friend and completely abandoned his purpose.

After this Aeneas, meeting the Cardinal of Pavia, said to him, "I hear that you too are with those who have decided to elect Rouen. Is this true?" He replied, "You have heard correctly. I have agreed to give him my vote so that I may not be left alone. For his victory is already certain; so many have declared for him." Aeneas said, "I thought you a different man from what I find you. Only see how much you have degenerated from your ancestors! Your father's brother (or was he your mother's?), Branda, Cardinal of Piacenza, when the papacy was beyond the mountains in Germany (for John XXIII, when he appointed the Council of Constance, had carried the Roman Curia across the Alps) never rested till he brought the Holy See back to Italy. It was owing to his diplomacy, devotion, and genius that on the withdrawal of the contestants for the papacy, Martin V, a Roman of the house of Colonna, was elected pope. Branda brought the Apostolic Curia back from Germany to Italy; you, his nephew, are going to transfer it from Italy to France. But Rouen will prefer his own nation to Italy and a Frenchman will be off to France with the supreme office.

"You say, 'He is under oath. He will not go outside this province without the decree of the senate and if he wishes to go, we will not consent.' What cardinal will dare oppose him when he is once seated on the apostolic throne? You will be the first, when you have secured some rich benefice, to say, 'Go where you will, Holy Father.' And what is our Italy without the Bishop of Rome? We still have the Apostleship though we have lost the Imperium, and in this one light we see light. Shall we be deprived of this with your sympathy, persuasion, help? A French pope will either go to France—and then our dear country is bereft of its splendor; or he will stay among us—and Italy, the queen of nations, will serve a foreign master, while we shall be the slaves of the French. The kingdom of Sicily will come into the hands of the French. The French will possess all the cities and strongholds of the Church. You might have taken warning from Calixtus, during whose papacy there was nothing the Catalans did not get. After trying the Catalans are you so eager to try the French? You will soon be sorry if you do! You will see the college filled with Frenchmen and the papacy will never again be wrested from them. Are you so dull that you do not realize that this will lay a yoke upon your nation forever?

"And what shall I say of this man's life? Are you not ashamed to entrust Christ's office to a slippery fellow who would sell his own soul? A fine bridegroom you are planning for the bride of Christ! You are trusting a lamb to a wolf. Where is your conscience? your zeal for justice? your common sense? Have you so far fallen below your true self? I suppose we have not often heard you say that it would be the Church's ruin if it fell into Rouen's hands? and that you would rather die than vote for this very man? What is the reason for this change? Has he suddenly been transformed from a demon to an angel of light? Or have you been changed from an angel of light to the devil, that you love his lust and filth and greed? What has become of your love for your country and your continual pro-testations that you preferred Italy above all other nations? I used to think that if everyone else fell away from devotion to her, you never would. You have failed me; nay, more, you have failed your-self and Italy, your country, unless you come to your senses."

The Cardinal of Pavia was stunned by these words and, overcome alike with grief and shame, he burst into tears. Then stifling his sobs he said, "I am ashamed, Aeneas. But what am I to do? I have given my promise. If I do not vote for Rouen, I shall be charged with treachery." Aeneas answered, "So far as I can see, it has come to the point where you will be guilty of treachery whichever way you turn. You now have to choose whether you prefer to betray Italy, your country, and the Church or the Bishop of Rouen." Convinced by these arguments Pavia decided it was less shameful to fail Rouen.

When Pietro, Cardinal of San Marco, learned of the conspiracy of the French and had lost hope of getting the papacy himself, actuated alike by patriotism and hatred of Rouen, he began to go to the Italian cardinals urging and warning them not to abandon their country; and he did not rest until he had gathered all the Italians except Colonna in the cell of the Cardinal of Genoa, revealed the conspiracy that had been made in the privies, and showed them that the Church would be ruined and Italy a slave forever, if Rouen should obtain the papacy. He implored them individually to show themselves men, to consult for the good of Mother Church and unhappy Italy, to put aside their enmities for one another and choose an Italian rather than a foreigner for pope. If they listened to him, they would prefer Aeneas to all others. There were present seven cardinals: Genoa, Orsini, Bologna, San Marco, Pavia, Siena, and Sant' Anastasia. All approved Pavia's words except Aeneas, who thought himself unworthy of so exalted an office.

The next day they went as usual to mass and then began the scrutiny. A golden chalice was placed on the altar and three cardinals, the Bishop of Ruthen, the Presbyter of Rouen, and the Deacon of Colonna, were set to watch it and see that there should be no cheating. The other cardinals took their seats and then, rising in order of rank and age, each approached the altar and deposited in the chalice a ballot on which was written the name of his choice for pope. When Aeneas came up to put in his ballot, Rouen, pale and trembling, said, "Look, Aeneas! I commend myself to you"— certainly a rash thing to say when it was not allowable to change what he had written. But ambition overcame prudence. Aeneas said, "Do you commend yourself to a worm like me?" and without another word he dropped his ballot in the cup and went back to his place.

When all had voted, a table was placed in the middle of the room and the three cardinals mentioned above turned out upon it the cupful of votes. Then they read aloud the ballots one after another and noted down the names written on them. And there was not a single cardinal who did not likewise make notes of those named, that there might be no possibility of trickery. This proved to be to Aeneas's advantage, for when the votes were counted and the teller, Rouen, announced that Aeneas had eight, though the rest said nothing about another man's loss, Aeneas did not allow himself to be defrauded. "Look more carefully at the ballots," he said to the teller, "for I have nine votes." The others agreed with him. Rouen said nothing, as if he had merely made a mistake.

This was the form of the ballot: The voter wrote with his own hand, "I, Peter (or John or whatever his name was) choose for pope Aeneas, Cardinal of Siena, and Jaime, Cardinal of Lisbon"; for it is permitted to vote for one or two or more, on the understanding that the one first named is the one preferred, but if he does not have enough votes to be elected, the next is to be counted in his place, that an agreement may more easily be reached. But a thing advantageous in itself some men pervert to base ends, as Latino Orsini did on that day. He named seven in the hope that those he named might be influenced by that good turn either to accede to him in that scrutiny or to vote for him in another; although he who has the reputation of a cheat does not gain much by tricks.

When the result of the scrutiny was made known, it was found, as we have said before, that nine cardinals (Genoa, Orsini, Lerida, Bologna, San Marco, Santi Quattro Coronati, Zamora, Pavia, and Portugal) had voted for Aeneas; the Cardinal of Rouen had only six votes, and the rest were far behind. Rouen was petrified when he saw himself so far outstripped by Aeneas and all the rest were amazed, for never within the memory of man had anyone polled as many as nine votes by scrutiny. Since no one had received enough votes for election, they decided to resume their seats and try the method that is called "by accession," to see if perhaps it might be possible to elect a pope that day. And here again Rouen indulged in empty hopes. All sat pale and silent in their places as if entranced. For some time no one spoke, no one opened his lips, no one moved any part of his body except the eyes, which kept glancing all about. It was a strange silence and a strange sight, men sitting there like their own statues; no sound to be heard, no movement to be seen. They remained thus for some moments, those inferior in rank waiting for their superiors to begin the accession.

Then Rodrigo, the Vice-Chancellor, rose and said, "I accede to the Cardinal of Siena," an utterance which was like a dagger in Rouen's heart, so pale did he turn. A silence followed and each man looking at his neighbor, began to indicate his sentiments by gestures. By this time it looked as if Aeneas would be pope and some, fearing this result, left the conclave, pretending physical needs, but really with the purpose of escaping the fate of that day. Those who thus withdrew were the Cardinals of Ruthen and San Sisto. However, as no one followed them, they soon returned. Then Jacopo, Cardinal of Sant' Anastasia, said, "I accede to the Cardinal of Siena." At this all appeared even more stunned, like people in a house shaken by unprecedented earthquakes, and lost the power of speech.

Aeneas now lacked but one vote, for twelve would elect a pope. Realizing this, Cardinal Prospero Colonna thought that he must get for himself the glory of announcing the pope. He rose and was about to pronounce his vote with the customary dignity, when he was seized by the Cardinals of Nicaea and Rouen and sharply rebuked for wishing to accede to Aeneas. When he persisted in his intention, they tried to get him out of the room by force, resorting even to such means to snatch the papacy from Aeneas. But Prospero, who, though he had voted for the Cardinal of Rouen on his ballot, was nevertheless bound to Aeneas by ties of old friendship, paid no attention to their abuse and empty threats. Turning to the other cardinals, he said, "I too accede to the Cardinal of Siena and I make him pope." When they heard this, the courage of the opposition failed and all their machinations were shattered.

All the cardinals immediately fell at Aeneas's feet and saluted him as Pope. Then they resumed their seats and ratified his election without a dissenting vote. At this point Bessarion, Cardinal of Nicaea, speaking for himself and for the others who had voted for the Cardinal of Rouen, said, "Your Holiness, we approve your election, which we do not doubt is of God. We thought before and still think that you are worthy of this office. The reason we did not vote for you was your infirmity. We thought your gout the one thing against you; for the Church needs an active man who has the physical strength to take long journeys and meet the dangers which we fear threaten us from the Turks. You on the contrary need rest. It was this consideration that won us to the side of the Cardinal of Rouen. If you were physically strong, there is no one we should have preferred. But, since God is satisfied, we must needs be satisfied too. God Himself, who has chosen you, will make good the defect in your feet and will not punish our ignorance. We revere you as Pope, we elect you again, so far as is in our power, and we will serve you faithfully."

Aeneas answered, "Your Eminence of Nicaea, your opinion of us, as we understand it, is much higher than our own, when you attribute to us no defect except that in our feet. We are not ignorant that our imperfection is more general and we realize that our failings, which might justly have caused us to be rejected as pope, are almost innumerable. As to any virtues which might raise us to this post, we know of none; and we should declare ourselves utterly unworthy and should refuse the honor offered us, if we did not fear the judgment of Him Who has called us. For what is done by two thirds of the sacred college, that is surely of the Holy Ghost, which may not be resisted. Therefore we obey the divine summons and we praise you, Your Eminence of Nicaea, and those who voted with you. If, following the dictates of your conscience, you thought we ought not to be elected as being inadequate, you will still be welcomed by us, who attribute our calling not to this man or that but to the whole college and to God Himself, from Whom cometh every good and perfect gift."

With these words he took off the garments he was wearing and put on the white tunic of Christ. When asked by what name he wished to be called, he answered, "Pius," and he was at once addressed as Pius II. Then after swearing to observe the capitulations that had been announced in the college two days before, he took his place by the altar and was again reverenced by the cardinals, who kissed his feet, hands, and cheek. After that the election of a pope was proclaimed to the people from a high window and it was announced that he who had been Cardinal of Siena was now Pope Pius II [August 19, 1458].

The attendants of the cardinals in the conclave plundered Aeneas's cell and meanly carried off all the plate (though it was very modest), his clothes, and his books; and the infamous rabble not only pillaged his house in the city but actually demolished it, taking away even the blocks of marble. Other cardinals, too, suffered losses, for while the people were waiting in suspense, various rumors got about and as now this cardinal, now that was reported elected, the crowd would rush to their houses and plunder them. The Cardinal of Genoa, whose name was mistaken for Siena, lost part of his possessions. Though many names were mentioned, none was received with enthusiasm except that of the Cardinal of Siena. When the cry arose that Rouen or Genoa or Lerida (for there were reports of them too) had been elected, all cast down their eyes and cursed the college. Only their personal friends were pleased; the rest shared the general sorrow. But when it was certain that Aeneas had been seated on Peter's throne, there was no one who did not rejoice. You might have seen not men only but the very animals and the buildings of the city exulting. Everywhere was heard laughter and expressions of joy and the cries of men shouting, "Siena! Siena! O happy Siena! Viva Siena!" Though the city was under arms and no one seemed to have confidence in anything but the sword, presently, when the people were told that the papacy had fallen to Aeneas, the aspect of the capital was completely changed. What had a little time before been the city of Mars all at once became the city, I will not say of Venus, the mother of that ancient Trojan Aeneas, but of Peace and Quiet, and joy and tranquility reigned everywhere.

Meantime the new Pope after taking a little refreshment was escorted to the Basilica of St. Peter and conducted to the high altar, under which lie the bodies of the blessed Apostles. Shortly after, he took his seat according to custom on the high throne and in the apostolic chair itself. There the cardinals and bishops and after them many of the people kissed his feet and reverenced him on his throne as Christ's Vicar. Then after a brief interval, when evening was coming on, they escorted him back to the palace. At nightfall fires blazed at every crossroad and on every tower; singing could be heard; neighbors called to neighbors; everywhere horns and trumpets blared and there was no spot in all the city which did not share in the general rejoicing. The older men said they had never seen such enthusiasm among the Roman populace.

The next night in a procession that reached from Hadrian's mausoleum to the Church of St. Peter the chief citizens of Rome on horseback and carrying lighted tapers went to the palace to greet the Pope.

Not only Rome but many states of Italy and many princes, when they heard of the accession of Pius, expressed the liveliest satisfaction, but the Sienese especially were elated, because their own citizen had been so exalted that he was now looked on as the first of all men on earth (though, to be sure, many who were enemies of the nobles grieved in their hearts). Ferrante, King of Sicily, welcomed the news because he realized that a friend of his father was now seated in the chair of St. Peter. Francesco Sforza, though he had expected a different pope, was nevertheless pleased to learn of the election of Aeneas, whom he had once received with honor in his camp, when he was attacking Milan. Borso, Duke of Modena, held military maneuvers and gave many conspicuous signs of his joy. His friendship with Aeneas dated from the time when he had received his dukedom from the Emperor Frederick, a favor in which Aeneas had had no small hand. He hoped that under the pontificate of Aeneas his fortunes and prestige would increase and therefore he saw to it that Ferrara and all his dominions should evince extravagant pleasure at the accession of the new pope. How many ways men have to get interest on their money! The Marquises of Mantua, Monferrato, and Saluzzo were equally delighted, for they all knew Aeneas and were his friends.

Only the Venetians and Florentines among the Italians were sorry to hear the news; the Venetians because Aeneas, when he was the Emperor's ambassador, had often seemed to them to speak overharshly in their Senate and to accuse them of tyranny; the Florentines because, as is the way of mankind with their neighbors, they hated the Sienese. They were so vexed at Aeneas's accession that when they were greeted by persons they met on the road with the customary words, "May God aid you," they answered indignantly, "He is busy with the Sienese, whom He is trying to bless!" Nevertheless the Venetians and the Florentines concealed their sentiments and like the other Italian powers sent to Rome very distinguished ambassadors to congratulate the new Pope and pledge him their obedience.

Among the Transalpine princes the Emperor Frederick was especially gratified, since it was from his service that Aeneas had been called to the cardinalate and had finally ascended the throne of St. Peter. All the Christian princes of Spain showed their satisfaction, but Scotland, Denmark, Poland, France, Hungary, and Cyprus were not pleased to hear that a friend of the Emperor had become Christ's

Vicar. The King of Bohemia was particularly distressed, for he realized that the Pope knew him for a heretic. Philip of Burgundy and Lodovico of Savoy were delighted with the elevation of their old friend Aeneas.

BOOK II

When Pius entered the Florentine territory, he was met at the town of Poggibonsi by ambassadors, the chief men of the city, who did honor to the Vicar of Christ in glowing words. This town is in our time of slight importance and lies in the valley of the Elsa River, but was once built on the lofty mountain which overlooks its present site. It was large and populous and difficult to storm. But since it took the side of the Ghibellines and often gave the Florentines a great deal of trouble, they first destroyed its walls, then razed it and moved it to the site just described. Here the Pope spent the night and the next day was met at San Casciano by new ambassadors, more numerous and more distinguished, who escorted him to the beautiful estate of a private citizen not far from the town, where he passed that night. The following day on his way to the Carthusian monastery he was met by the lords of Faenza, Forli, and Imola and soon after by Galeazzo Sforza, the eldest son of Francesco Sforza, Duke of Milan. This handsome youth was not yet sixteen, but his character, eloquence, and ability were such that he exhibited a wisdom greater than that of a grown man. In his expression and bearing there was the dignity befitting a prince; his extemporaneous speeches could hardly have been equaled by another after long preparation; there was nothing childish or trivial in his conduct. It was astounding to hear the sentiments of an old man issuing from the lips of a lad and to listen to a beardless boy giving utterance to the ideas of a graybeard. His father had sent him with a splendid and magnificently accoutered escort of five hundred horsemen from Milan to Florence and thence to meet the Pope. Encountering Pius at the third milestone a little beyond the Certosa, Galeazzo dismounted and kissed the holy feet according to custom.

Luncheon was laid for the Pope in the monastery and after it he made haste toward the city, where he was met about two stades

outside the gate by the chiefs of the Guelfs and at the gate itself
by the Gonfalonier and many other magistrates, called the Lord
Priors, who greeted the Pope humbly, kissed his feet, and com-
mended to him the city and the people. The Pope because of his
gout could not ride on horseback but was carried in a gold chair
on the shoulders of his attendants. Just as he entered the city, after
the priests carrying the sacred relics had received his blessing and
had advanced to take their places at the head of the procession,
Sigismondo Malatesta and the other vicars of the Church, whom I
have mentioned above, raised the Pope's chair on their shoulders
and carried their master some distance, Sigismondo exclaiming
indignantly, "See to what we lords of cities have been brought!"
Galeazzo, who was too short and somewhat weak in the legs, thought
he could not help with the weight, yet laid his hand on the chair
as desiring to appear to be one of the bearers. The chief men of
the city walked on either side. The bearers were changed at fixed
intervals and the most distinguished citizens claimed a part in this
service. When Galeazzo had walked a short distance, he remounted
at the Pope's command and, soon after, the vicars of the Church
did likewise. The city was full of people, both citizens and outsiders.
From the neighboring towns and from the country they had
gathered from all sides to see the new Pope. The women were
richly dressed and there was a marvelous variety of costumes in both
domestic and foreign style, but their whitened faces clearly betrayed the use of cosmetics. The Pope visited the church of the
Reparata and the baptistery of San Giovanni and at both blessed
the people. He was lodged at Santa Maria Novella, where Martin
and Eugenius had been entertained before him.

Florence, once called Fluentia from the river Arno which "flows"
through it, is now the capital of Tuscany. It was built on the ruins
of Faesulae, which was destroyed by Totila, King of the Goths.
The city subjugated Volterra, Pistoia, Arezzo, Cortona, and Pisa;
deprived Lucca of much of her territory; inflicted great disasters on
the Sienese, at whose hands she herself sometimes suffered. She
often opposed the German emperors. Henry VII [c. 1269-1313;
Roman Emperor, who in 1310 tried to reunite Germany and Italy
by conquest,] pitched his camp before her walls and laid strenuous
siege to the city, which he would certainly have taken had he not

been called to Naples to fight King Robert and on his way there
with part of his forces died from poison at Buonconvento, as I
have before related. . . . The Dukes of Milan have cherished the
bitterest hatred against the Florentines and have inflicted heavy
losses upon them, though not without damage to themselves.
Francesco Sforza made himself Duke of Milan with their help and
was their fast friend. The kings of Naples were regarded by them
now as friends, now as foes, and at one time were masters of the
city, which was also once ruled by the Duke of Athens. When the
latter was finally expelled, the people asserted their independence,
though they first began to know real slavery when they believed
themselves free, having driven out one master only to admit many.
The city has often been racked by civil war, while the upper classes
fought together for the mastery.

The most distinguished Florentines of our time have been thought
to be Palla Strozzi, Niccolò Uzzano, and Rodolfo Peruzzi. Palla
surpassed all others in wealth, Niccolò in wisdom, Rodolfo in military prowess. Against these men Cosimo de' Medici stirred up a
faction and as a result he was banished and remained for some
time in exile. Uzzano was already dead. Then when Pope Eugenius
was residing in Florence, amid the strife of the various parties
Cosimo returned and in the general confusion cowed his opponents
and regained his old prestige. He drove into exile Rodolfo and
Palla together with numerous other citizens and they never returned, though Rodolfo, enlisting the services of Niccolò Piccinino
against his country, raided and plundered the district of Mugellana.
He afterward died in exile. Palla endured adversity cheerfully, occupying himself till he was very old in the study of philosophy at
Padua, where he died when nearly ninety, a man who had not
deserved banishment at the hands of his countrymen.

Cosimo, having thus disposed of his rivals, proceeded to admin-
ister the state at his pleasure and amassed such wealth as I should
think Croesus could hardly have possessed. In Florence he built a
palace fit for a king; he restored some churches and erected others;
he founded the splendid monastery of San Marco and stocked its
library richly with Greek and Latin manuscripts; he decorated his
villas magnificently. It was beginning to look as if by these noble
works he had overcome envy, but the people always hate superior

worth and there were some who asserted that Cosimo's tyranny was intolerable and tried in every way to thwart his projects; some also hurled insults at him.

The time was now at hand for making a valuation of the property of each citizen. The Florentines call this process *catasto;* the Sienese, *libra.* By it the magistrates learn the resources of the citizens and can thus apportion the burdens fairly among them. Cosimo urged a new *catasto;* his opponents were against it. Therefore it was decided to call a *parlamento.* While it was assembling, armed men, gathered from all quarters at Cosimo's orders, surrounded the piazza and made it clear that any who objected to his plans would do so at their peril. The *catasto* was voted under fear of armed force and some of the citizens who had opposed it were banished, others fined. After this Cosimo was refused nothing. He was regarded as the arbiter of war and peace, the regulator of law; not so much a citizen as the master of his city. Political councils were held at his house; the magistrates he nominated were elected; he was king in all but name and state. Therefore when Pius once asked the Bishop of Orta what he thought about Florence and he replied that it was a pity so beautiful a woman had not a husband, the Pope said, "Yes, but she has a paramour," meaning that she had a tyrant instead of a king and referring to Cosimo, who like an unlawful lord of the city was grinding the people with cruel slavery. During Pius' stay in Florence Cosimo was ill or perhaps, as many believed, he pretended to be ill that he might not have to wait on the Pope.

Cosimo's ancestors came to Florence from Mugello. His father Giovanni, who became a client of the Medici, took the name of that family. He had left a great fortune to his sons, Cosimo and Lorenzo, and Cosimo had increased it to an incredible degree, extending his business transactions over all Europe and trading even as far as Egypt. He was of fine physique and more than average height; his expression and manner of speech were mild; he was more cultured than merchants usually are and had some knowledge of Greek; his mind was keen and always alert; his spirit was neither cowardly nor brave; he easily endured toil and hunger and he often passed whole nights without sleep. Nothing went on in Italy that he did not know; indeed it was his advice that guided the policy of many cities and princes. Nor were foreign events a secret to him,

for he had correspondents among his business connections all over
the world, who kept him informed by frequent letters of what was
going on around them. Toward the end of his life he suffered from
gout, a disease which he lived to see passed on to his sons and grandsons. At the time the Pope was in Florence he [Cosimo] was more
than seventy years old.

At this time there passed away in the Lord, Antonino, Archbishop of Florence, a member of the Order of Preaching Friars and
a man whose memory deserves to live. He conquered avarice,
trampled on pride, was utterly unacquainted with lust, and most
abstemious in food and drink; he did not yield to anger or envy or
any other passion. He was a brilliant theologian; he wrote several
books which are praised by scholars; he was a popular preacher,
though he inveighed against sin with the utmost violence; he re-
formed the morals of clergy and laity; he strove earnestly to settle
quarrels; he did his best to clear the city of feuds; the revenues of
his church he distributed among Christ's poor; to his relatives and
connections, unless they were very needy, he gave nothing. He used
only glass and clay dishes; he wished his household (which was very
small) to be contented with little and to live according to the precepts of philosophy. When he died he was given a splendid public
funeral. At his house nothing was found except the mule on which
he used to ride and some cheap furniture; the poor had had everything else. The whole state believed that he had passed to a life of
bliss—nor can we think their belief unfounded.

In former ages there have been many illustrious Florentines
whose names are known even today, but most illustrious of all was
Dante Alighieri, whose great poem with its noble description of
Heaven, Hell, and Purgatory breathes a wisdom almost divine,
though, being but mortal, he sometimes erred. Next to him was
Francesco Petrarca, whose equal would be hard to find if his Latin
works were comparable to those he wrote in Italian. The third
place I should not go wrong in assigning to Giovanni Boccaccio,
though he was a little more frivolous and his style was not highly
polished. After him comes Coluccio, whose prose and verse suited
his own age but seem rough to ours. He was Chancellor of Florence,
and Galeazzo, Duke of Milan, used to say that Coluccio's pen did
him more harm than thirty troops of the cavalry of the Florentines,

who were then the enemies of Milan. For Coluccio was a shrewd man and, though his style lacked elegance, yet he had a thorough understanding of the general truths by which men are stirred and in his writing he handled them most skillfully. After several years he was succeeded in office by Leonardo, who was born in Arezzo but had been made a Florentine citizen. He was deeply versed in Greek and Latin and his eloquence was almost Ciceronian. He made a brilliant reputation by his many translations from Greek into Latin. Almost his equal in prose and his superior in verse was Carlo, who was also an Aretine by birth but a Florentine by courtesy. Poggio too was a famous citizen of Florence. After he had served for some time as papal secretary and had written several distinguished works, he finally returned to his native city, where he was made Chancellor and ended his days among his own kinsmen. A great many more men might be mentioned by whose abilities the power and prestige of Florence have been increased.

The admirers of Florence call attention not only to her illustrious citizens but to the size of the city (which is surpassed in all Italy by Rome alone), the lofty and extraordinarily thick walls which encircle it, the elegance of the streets and squares which are not only wide but straight, the magnificent churches, and the splendid towering palaces, both public and private. But among all the buildings none is more deserving of mention than the church of the Reparata, the dome of which is nearly as large as that which we admire at Rome in the temple of Agrippa called the Pantheon. Next comes the palace of the Priors and third that built by Cosimo. They admire too the sanctuary of St. John the Baptist and the church of San Lorenzo (also built by Cosimo). They mention the bridges which unite the city cut in two by the Arno and the numerous population and the costumes of both men and women and the shops of all sorts and the great estates and the splendid luxurious villas near the city erected at no less expense than the city itself, and finally the quick wits of the citizens, though they most excel in trade, which philosophers think sordid. They seem too bent on making money, and, therefore, when the chief men of the city had collected fourteen thousand ducats from the people to honor the Pope, they kept the greater part for the city and used part to support Galeazzo and his retinue. They spent very little on entertaining the Pope nor did they lay out much on lavish spectacles, though they brought lions into the piazza to fight with horses and other animals and arranged tournaments in which much more wine was drunk than blood spilled.

The Pope remained a week, in the course of which Sigismondo Malatesta [lord of Rimini, a principality on the Adriatic northeast of Florence] earnestly besought him to arbitrate between him and Ferrante, King of Sicily, who was making war against him.

Sigismondo, of the noble family of the Malatesta but illegitimate, was very vigorous in body and mind, eloquent, and gifted with great military ability. He had a thorough knowledge of history and no slight acquaintance with philosophy. Whatever he attempted he seemed born for, but the evil part of his character had the upper hand. He was such a slave to avarice that he was ready not only to plunder but to steal. His lust was so unbridled that he violated his daughters and his sons-in-law. He outdid all barbarians in cruelty. His bloody hand inflicted terrible punishments on innocent and guilty alike. He oppressed the poor, plundered the rich, spared neither widows nor orphans. No one felt safe under his rule. Wealth or a beautiful wife or handsome children were enough to cause a man to be accused of crime. He hated priests and despised religion. He had no belief in another world and thought the soul died with the body. Nevertheless he built at Rimini a splendid church dedicated to St. Francis, though he filled it so full of pagan works of art that it seemed less a Christian sanctuary than a temple of heathen devil-worshippers. In it he erected for his mistress a tomb of magnificent marble and exquisite workmanship with an inscription in the pagan style as follows, "Sacred to the deified Isotta." The two wives he had married before he took Isotta for his mistress he killed one after the other with the sword or poison.

He showed himself a perjurer and traitor to Alfonso, King of Sicily, and his son Ferrante. He broke his word to Francesco, Duke of Milan, to the Venetians, the Florentines and the Sienese. Repeatedly too he tricked the Church of Rome. Finally, when there was no one left in Italy for him to betray, he went on to the French, who allied themselves with him out of hatred for Pope Pius but fared no better than the other princes. When his subjects once begged him to retire at last to a peaceful life and spare his country, which had so often been exposed to pillage on his account, he replied, "Go and be of good courage; never while I live shall you have peace."

Such was Sigismondo, intolerant of peace, a devotee of pleasure, able to endure any hardship, and greedy for war. Of all men who have ever lived or ever will live he was the worst scoundrel, the disgrace of Italy and the infamy of our times. Alfonso hired him for a large sum to fight for him in the war he was waging with the Florentines. Sigismondo however, attracted by a new price, went over to the Florentines and turned his arms against Alfonso, alleging as a reason for his perfidy that his stipend had not all been paid on time. This was a heavy blow to the King, who now had to face an enemy whom he had hired to be his champion. There is no doubt that the treachery of Sigismondo was the salvation of the Florentine cause and so, on the conclusion of a general peace and an alliance among the princes of Italy, Sigismondo, as well as the Genoese and Astorre of Faenza, was excluded, the King reserving the right to declare war on those who had broken their oaths and betrayed him. Alfonso therefore equipped a powerful fleet against the Genoese and in the last year of his life (which was also Pope Calixtus' last) he sent against Sigismondo a large army commanded by Piccinino, the son of Niccolò, a step enthusiastically supported by Federigo of Urbino, who had his own reasons for hating Sigismondo. The war dragged on for some time, not only during Alfonso's life but after his death, since his son was as enraged at Sigismondo as his father had been. The tyrant's subjects suffered for their master's guilt and the poor had their houses burned over their heads because of the arrogance of an impious scoundrel. A region famous through all Italy, which, though subject to the tyrant, belonged legally to the Church of Rome, was being ravaged and laid waste. Pope Pius, deploring this fact, included among the conditions imposed on Ferrante when he was invested with the kingdom of Sicily, that he should make peace with Sigismondo on terms dictated by the Pope himself. But after Pius had recovered Assisi, his freedom to dictate was restricted and it was decided that peace should be made on certain specific conditions; or, if Sigismondo would not consent to this, they should annul the mutual agreement made when the Pope was a free agent. It was settled that this should

not continue in force later than the month of February, but afterward the time was extended to include March and then April.

When Pius was at Florence only four days of this period were
left and the King's agents were not there to state his case. There
were present however ambassadors from Federigo of Urbino and
Jacopo Piccinino, to whom the King had delegated the matter. The
Pope directed four cardinals to hear the two parties and to reconcile them, but they were unsuccessful. Then the Pope in person
heard the arguments and claims of both sides and there was no
doubt that Sigismondo was guilty of treachery. It was therefore
decided that he should pay for his offense with money or, if he had
none, should pledge his castles. But since much was demanded in
the King's [Ferrante, King of Sicily] name and Sigismondo offered
little, the case seemed to be almost desperate. The ambassadors
asserted that victory was theirs; Sigismondo declared he was not
yet beaten and that he would suffer anything rather than surrender
what was demanded. In the midst of his insolent blustering the Pope
said to him, "Be quiet. We are concerned for your house, not for
you. It is not you but your subjects whom we pity, since your
actions give you no claim to consideration and no punishment is
adequate for your crimes. Your life heretofore has been such that
no penalty too severe for your wickedness could be devised. No
matter how long you talk in your own defense, there is no one who
does not think you a traitor to Alfonso." Sigismondo, terrified at
hearing this, consented to terms that seemed likely to be acceptable,
but the other side with the insolence of the victor objected and
would consent to no compromise.

The Pope, though he had the power to make any decision he
pleased about Sigismondo, nevertheless thought it disgraceful to
consider victory rather than justice and for a long time strove to
settle the quarrel to the satisfaction of both sides. When he failed,
he released both the King and Sigismondo from their agreement,
uncertain whether a war of this kind or peace was more advantageous for the Church, since it was common knowledge that Piccinino could not keep quiet and if he were freed from the war with
Sigismondo, he would probably turn his arms against the Church.
Pius therefore came to the conclusion that it was God's will that
the peace could not be arranged. The Florentines agreed with him

and rejoiced that the day had come when a scoundrel should at last be punished as he deserved.

The Pope slept the first night after leaving Florence in a very beautiful villa in the Mugello belonging to Cosimo. The next day he crossed the summit of the Apennines and spent the night in the town of Firenzuola. On leaving Firenzuola the Pope crossed another ridge of the Apennines with considerable toil and difficulty and arrived at Pianoro, having met the Bolognese envoys a little beyond Caprenno, which is on the boundary between the Florentine and Bolognese territories.

GIOVANNI PICO
DELLA MIRANDOLA

Giovanni Pico was born into the ruling family of the northern county of Mirandola in 1463, and died in Florence in 1494. One of the most precocious philosophical talents of all time, he had produced a number of significant and promising works before his premature death. Though known most widely as a philosopher in the Platonic tradition, he showed considerable gifts as a poet in Latin and Italian, had an elegant epistolary style in the humanist tradition, a deep knowledge of Scripture that found expression in several commentaries, and an interest in astrology, which he attacked in a lengthy and very influential posthumous work.

As a philosopher, Pico has been generally regarded as a syncretist, one who attempts to reconcile those elements in every available philosophical and theological system that are judged to be true. This syncretistic impulse was present in many Renaissance philosophers, who faced the problem of recognizing great strengths in apparently contradictory systems inherited from the past. But Pico was the most ambitious of the syncretists, for it was his intention to discover and reconcile the valid elements not only of Christianity and of Greek and Roman thought, but also of Arabic philosophy and the mystical texts of Jewish theology known as *Cabala*. Unlike most humanists and Florentine Platonists, and perhaps owing in part to his own scholastic training in the University of Paris, Pico complicated his task immensely by accepting the Aristotelian philosophical tradition as a vital element in his projected system. Elements from all these sources and others may be found in the nine hundred theses which Pico published in Rome in

1486, as a subject for scholarly debate. But this disputation never occurred, because Pope Innocent VIII prohibited it, and appointed a commission to pass upon the orthodoxy of the theses, thirteen of which were condemned as heretical.

Pico's *Oration on the Dignity of Man* (simply called *Oration* by him) seems to have been intended as an introductory address for the disputation which never took place. In it, he sets forth a conception of man's place in the universe which seems to express in philosophical terms many of the attitudes and assumptions of humanists from Petrarch onward. He also undertakes to explain and defend his attempt at a synthesis of the truths contained in his many sources, in a way which exemplifies his nearly universal knowledge, his boundless energies, and his unusual tolerance. ("Oration on the Dignity of Man," translated by Elizabeth L. Forbes. From *The Renaissance Philosophy of Man,* edited by Ernst Cassirer, Paul Oskar Kristeller, and John Herman Randall, Jr. Chicago: University of Chicago Press, 1948, pp. 223-54. Copyright 1948 by The University of Chicago. Reprinted by permission of University of Chicago Press.)

From *Oration on the Dignity of Man*

I have read in the records of the Arabians, reverend Fathers, that Abdala the Saracen, when questioned as to what on this stage of the world, as it were, could be seen most worthy of wonder, replied: "There is nothing to be seen more wonderful than man." In agreement with this opinion is the saying of Hermes Trismegistus: "A great miracle, Asclepius, is man." But when I weighed the reason for these maxims, the many grounds for the excellence of human nature reported by many men failed to satisfy me—that man is the intermediary between creatures; the intimate of the gods; the king of the lower beings; by the acuteness of his senses, by the discernment of his reason, and by the light of his intelligence the interpreter of nature; the interval between fixed eternity and fleeting time; and (as the Persians say) the bond, nay, rather, the marriage song of the world, on David's testimony but little lower than the angels. Admittedly great though these reasons be, they are not the principal grounds, that is, those which may rightfully claim for themselves the privilege of the highest admiration. For why should we not admire more the angels themselves and the blessed choirs of heaven? At last it seems to me I have come to understand why man is the most fortunate of creatures and consequently worthy of all admiration and what precisely is that rank which is his lot in the universal chain of Being—a rank to be envied not only by brutes but even by the stars and by minds beyond this world. It is a matter past faith and a wondrous one. Why should it not be? For it is on this very account that man is rightly called and judged a great miracle and a wonderful creature indeed.

But hear, Fathers, exactly what this rank is and, as friendly auditors, conformably to your kindness, do me this favor. God the Father, the supreme Architect, had already built this cosmic home we behold, the most sacred temple of His godhead, by the laws of His mysterious wisdom. The region above the heavens He had adorned with Intelligences, the heavenly spheres He had quickened with eternal souls, and the excrementary and filthy parts of the lower world He had filled with a multitude of animals of every kind. But, when the work was finished, the Craftsman kept wishing that there were someone to ponder the plan of so great a work, to love its beauty, and to wonder at its vastness. Therefore, when everything was done (as Moses and Timaeus bear witness), He finally took thought concerning the creation of man. But there was not among His archetypes that from which He could fashion a new offspring, nor was there in His treasurehouses anything which He might bestow on His new son as an inheritance, nor was there in the seats of all the world a place where the latter might sit to contemplate the universe. All was now complete; all things had been assigned to the highest, the middle, and the lowest orders. But in its final creation it was not the part of the Father's power to fail as though exhausted. It was not the part of His wisdom to waver in a needful matter through poverty of counsel. It was not the part of His kindly love that he who was to praise God's divine generosity in regard to others should be compelled to condemn it in regard to himself.

At last the best of artisans ordained that that creature to whom He had been able to give nothing proper to himself should have joint possession of whatever had been peculiar to each of the dif-

ferent kinds of being. He therefore took man as a creature of inde-
terminate nature and, assigning him a place in the middle of the
world, addressed him thus:

> Neither a fixed abode nor a form that is thine alone nor any function
> peculiar to thyself have we given thee, Adam, to the end that accord-
> ing to thy longing and according to thy judgment thou mayest have
> and possess what abode, what form, and what functions thou thyself
> shalt desire. The nature of all other beings is limited and constrained
> within the bounds of laws prescribed by Us. Thou, constrained by no
> limits, in accordance with thine own free will, in whose hand We have
> placed thee, shalt ordain for thyself the limits of thy nature. We have
> set thee at the world's center that thou mayest from thence more easily
> observe whatever is in the world. We have made thee neither of heaven
> nor of earth, neither mortal nor immortal, so that with freedom of
> choice and with honor, as though the maker and molder of thyself, thou
> mayest fashion thyself in whatever shape thou shalt prefer. Thou shalt
> have the power to degenerate into the lower forms of life, which are
> brutish. Thou shalt have the power, out of thy soul's judgment, to be
> reborn into the higher forms, which are divine.

O supreme generosity of God the Father, O highest and most
marvelous felicity of man! To him it is granted to have whatever
he chooses, to be whatever he wills. Beasts as soon as they are born
(so says Lucilius) bring with them from their mother's womb all
they will ever possess. Spiritual beings, either from the beginning or
soon thereafter, become what they are to be for ever and ever. On
man when he came into life the Father conferred the seeds of all
kinds and the germs of every way of life. Whatever seeds each man
cultivates will grow to maturity and bear in him their own fruit.
If they be vegetative, he will be like a plant. If sensitive, he will
become brutish. If rational, he will grow into a heavenly being. If
intellectual, he will be an angel and the son of God. And if, happy
in the lot of no created thing, he withdraws into the center of his
own unity, his spirit, made one with God, in the solitary darkness
of God, who is set above all things, shall surpass them all. Who
would not admire this our chameleon? Or who could more greatly
admire aught else whatever? It is man who Asclepius of Athens [a
Greek mystical philosopher], arguing from his mutability of charac-

ter and from his self-transforming nature, on just grounds says was symbolized by Proteus in the mysteries. Hence those metamorphoses renowned among the Hebrews and the Pythagoreans. . . .

Are there any who would not admire man, who is, in the sacred writings of Moses and the Christians, not without reason described sometimes by the name of "all flesh," sometimes by that of "every creature," inasmuch as he himself molds, fashions, and changes himself into the form of all flesh and into the character of every creature? For this reason the Persian Euanthes, in describing the Chaldaean theology, writes that man has no semblance that is inborn and his very own but many that are external and foreign to him; whence this saying of the Chaldaeans: "Hanorish tharah sharinas," that is, "Man is a being of varied, manifold, and inconstant nature." But why do we emphasize this? To the end that after we have been born to this condition—that we can become what we will—we should understand that we ought to have special care to this, that it should never be said against us that, although born to a privileged position, we failed to recognize it and became like unto wild animals and senseless beasts of burden, but that rather the saying of Asaph the prophet should apply: "Ye are all angels and sons of the Most High," and that we may not, by abusing the most indulgent generosity of the Father, make for ourselves that freedom of choice He has given into something harmful instead of salutary. Let a certain holy ambition invade our souls, so that, not content with the mediocre, we shall pant after the highest and (since we may if we wish) toil with all our strength to obtain it.

Let us disdain earthly things, despise heavenly things, and, finally, esteeming less whatever is of the world, hasten to that court which is beyond the world and nearest to the Godhead. There, as the sacred mysteries relate, Seraphim, Cherubim, and Thrones hold the first places; let us, incapable of yielding to them, and intolerant of a lower place, emulate their dignity and their glory. If we have willed it, we shall be second to them in nothing.

But how shall we go about it, and what in the end shall we do? Let us consider what they do, what sort of life they lead. If we also come to lead that life (for we have the power), we shall then equal their good fortune. The Seraph burns with the fire of love. The

Cherub glows with the splendor of intelligence. The Throne stands by the steadfastness of judgment. Therefore, if in giving ourselves over to the active life we have after due consideration undertaken the care of the lower beings, we shall be strengthened with the firm stability of Thrones. If, unoccupied by deeds, we pass our time in the leisure of contemplation, considering the Creator in the creature and the creature in the Creator, we shall be all ablaze with Cherubic light. If we long with love for the Creator himself alone, we shall speedily flame up with His consuming fire into a Seraphic likeness. Above the Throne, that is, above the just judge, God sits as Judge of the ages. Above the Cherub, that is, above him who contemplates, God flies, and cherishes him, as it were, in watching over him. For the spirit of the Lord moves upon the waters, the waters, I say, which are above the firmament and which in *Job* praise the Lord with hymns before dawn. Whoso[ever] is a Seraph, that is, a lover, is in God and God in him, nay, rather, God and himself are one. Great is the power of Thrones, which we attain in using judgment, and most high the exaltation of Seraphs, which we attain in loving.

But by what means is one able either to judge or to love things unknown? Moses loved a God whom he saw and, as judge, administered among the people what he had first beheld in contemplation upon the mountain. Therefore, the Cherub as intermediary by his own light makes us ready for the Seraphic fire and equally lights the way to the judgment of the Thrones. This is the bond of the first minds, the Palladian order, the chief of contemplative philosophy. This is the one for us first to emulate, to court, and to understand; the one from whence we may be rapt to the heights of love and descend, well taught and well prepared, to the functions of active life. But truly it is worthwhile, if our life is to be modeled on the example of the Cherubic life, to have before our eyes and clearly understood both its nature and its quality and those things which are the deeds and the labor of Cherubs. But since it is not permitted us to attain this through our own efforts, we who are but flesh and know of the things of earth, let us go to the ancient fathers who, inasmuch as they were familiar and conversant with these matters, can give sure and altogether trustworthy testimony. Let us consult the Apostle Paul, the chosen vessel, as to what **he** saw the hosts of Cherubim doing when he was himself exalted to the third heaven. He will answer, according to the interpretation of Dionysius, that he saw them being purified, then being illuminated, and at last being made perfect. Let us also, therefore, by emulating the Cherubic way of life on earth, by taming the impulses of our passions with moral science, by dispelling the darkness of reason with dialectic, and by, so to speak, washing away the filth of ignorance and vice, cleanse our soul, so that her passions may not rave at random nor her reason through heedlessness ever be deranged.

Then let us fill our well-prepared and purified soul with the light of natural philosophy, so that we may at last perfect her in the knowledge of things divine. And lest we be satisfied with those of our faith, let us consult the patriarch Jacob, whose form gleams carved on the throne of glory. Sleeping in the lower world but keeping watch in the upper, the wisest of fathers will advise us. But he will advise us through a figure (in this way everything was wont to come to those men) that there is a ladder extending from the lowest earth to the highest heaven, divided in a series of many steps, with the Lord seated at the top, and angels in contemplation ascending and descending over them alternately by turns.

If this is what we must practice in our aspiration to the angelic way of life, I ask: "Who will touch the ladder of the Lord either with fouled foot or with unclean hands?" As the sacred mysteries have it, it is impious for the impure to touch the pure. But what are these feet? What these hands? Surely the foot of the soul is that most contemptible part by which the soul rests on matter as on the soil of the earth; I mean the nourishing and feeding power, the tinder of lust, and the teacher of pleasurable weakness. Why should we not call the hands of the soul its irascible power, which struggles on its behalf as the champion of desire and as plunderer seizes in the dust and sun what desire will devour slumbering in the shade? These hands, these feet, that is, all the sentient part whereon resides the attraction of the body which, as they say, by wrenching the neck holds the soul in check, lest we be hurled down from the ladder as impious and unclean, let us bathe in moral philosophy as if in a living river. Yet this will not be enough if we wish to be companions of the angels going up and down on Jacob's ladder, unless we have first been well fitted and instructed to be promoted duly from step to step, to stray nowhere from the stairway, and to engage in the alternate comings and goings. Once we have achieved this by the art of discourse or reasoning, then, inspired by the Cherubic spirit, using philosophy through the steps of the ladder, that is, of nature, and penetrating all things from center to center, we shall sometimes descend, with titanic force rending the unity like Osiris into many parts, and we shall sometimes ascend, with the force of Phoebus collecting the parts like the limbs of Osiris into a unity, until, resting at last in the bosom of the Father who is above the ladder, we shall be made perfect with the felicity of theology.

Let us also inquire of the just Job, who entered into a life-covenant with God before he himself was brought forth into life, what the most high God requires above all in those tens of hundreds of thousands who attend him. He will answer that it is peace, in accord with what we read in him: "He maketh peace in his high places." And since the middle order expounds to the lower orders the counsel of the highest order, let Empedocles the philosopher expound to us the words of Job the theologian. He indicates to us a twofold nature present in our souls, by one side of which we are raised on high to the heavenly regions, and by the other side plunged downward into the lower, through strife and friendship or through war and peace, as he witnesses in the verses in which he makes complaint that he is being driven into the sea, himself goaded by strife and discord into the semblance of a madman and a fugitive from the gods.

Surely, Fathers, there is in us a discord many times as great; we have at hand wars grievous and more than civil, wars of the spirit which, if we dislike them, if we aspire to that peace which may so raise us to the sublime that we shall be established among the exalted of the Lord, only philosophy will entirely allay and subdue in us. In the first place, if our man but ask a truce of his enemies, moral philosophy will check the unbridled inroads of the many-sided beast and the leonine passions of wrath and violence. If we then take wiser counsel with ourselves and learn to desire the security of everlasting peace, it will be at hand and will generously fulfill our prayers. After both beasts are felled like a sacrificed sow, it will confirm an inviolable compact of holiest peace between flesh and spirit. Dialectic will appease the tumults of reason made confused and anxious by inconsistencies of statement and sophisms of syllogisms. Natural philosophy will allay the strife and differences of opinion which vex, distract, and wound the spirit from all sides. But she will so assuage them as to compel us to remember that, according to Heraclitus, nature was begotten from war, that it was on this account repeatedly called "strife" by Homer, and that it is not, therefore, in the power of natural philosophy to give us in nature a true quiet and unshaken peace but that this is the function and privilege of her mistress, that is, of holiest theology. She will show us the way and as comrade lead us to her who, seeing us hastening from afar, will exclaim "Come to me, ye who have labored. Come and I will restore you. Come to me, and I will give you peace, which the world and nature cannot give you."

When we have been so soothingly called, so kindly urged, we shall fly up with winged feet, like earthly Mercuries, to the embraces of our blessed mother and enjoy that wished-for peace, most holy peace, indivisible bond, of one accord in the friendship through which all rational souls not only shall come into harmony in the one mind which is above all minds, but shall in some ineffable way become altogether one. This is that friendship which the Pythagoreans say is the end of all philosophy. This is that peace which God creates in his heavens, which the angels descending to earth proclaimed to men of good will, that through it men might ascend to heaven and become angels. Let us wish this peace for our friends, for our century. Let us wish it for every home into which we go; let us wish it for our own soul, that through it she shall herself be made the house of God, and to the end that as soon as she has cast out her uncleanness through moral philosophy and dialectic, adorned herself with manifold philosophy as with the splendor of a courtier, and crowned the pediments of her doors with the garlands of theology, the King of Glory may descend and, coming with his Father, make his stay with her. If she show herself worthy of so great a guest, she shall, by the boundless mercy which is his, in golden raiment like a wedding gown, and surrounded by a varied throng of sciences, receive her beautiful guest not merely as a guest but as a spouse from whom she will never be parted. She will desire rather to be parted from her own people and, forgetting her father's house and herself, will desire to die in herself in order to live in her spouse, in whose sight surely the death of his saints is precious—death, I say, if we must call death that fulness of life, the consideration of which wise men have asserted to be the aim of philosophy.

Let us also cite Moses himself, but little removed from the springing abundance of the holy and unspeakable wisdom by whose nectar the angels are made drunk. Let us hearken to the venerable judge in these words proclaiming laws to us who are dwellers in the desert loneliness of this body [cf. *Exod.* 26:14; 36:19; 39:33]:

> Let those who, as yet unclean, still need moral philosophy, live with the people outside the tabernacle under the sky, meanwhile purifying themselves like the priests of Thessaly. Let those who have already ordered their conduct be received into the sanctuary but not quite yet touch the holy vessels; let them first like zealous Levites in the service of dialectic minister to the holy things of philosophy. Then when they have been admitted even to these, let them now behold the many-colored robe of the higher palace of the Lord, that is to say, the stars; let them now behold the heavenly candlestick divided into seven lights; let them now behold the fur tent, that is, the elements, in the priesthood of philosophy, so that when they are in the end, through the favor of theological sublimity, granted entrance into the inner part of the temple, they may rejoice in the glory of the Godhead with no veil before his image.

This surely Moses commands us and, in commanding, summons, urges, and encourages us by means of philosophy to prepare ourselves a way, while we can, to the heavenly glory to come.

But indeed not only the Mosaic and Christian mysteries but also the theology of the ancients show us the benefits and value of the liberal arts, the discussion of which I am about to undertake. For what else did the degrees of the initiates observed in the mysteries of the Greeks mean? For they arrived at a perception of the mysteries when they had first been purified through those expiatory sciences, as it were, moral philosophy and dialectic. What else can that perception possibly be than an interpretation of occult nature by means of philosophy? Then at length to those who were so disposed came that ΕΠΟΠΤΕΙΑ, that is to say, the observation of things divine by the light of theology. Who would not long to be initiated into such sacred rites? Who would not desire, by neglecting all human concerns, by despising the goods of fortune, and by disregarding those of the body, to become the guest of the gods while yet living on earth, and, made drunk by the nectar of eternity, to be endowed with the gifts of immortality though still a mortal being? Who would not wish to be so inflamed with those Socratic frenzies sung by Plato in the *Phaedrus*, that, by the oarage of feet and wings escaping speedily from hence, that is, from a world set on evil, he might be borne on the fastest of courses to the heavenly Jerusalem? Let us be driven, Fathers, let us be driven by the frenzies of Socrates, that they may so throw us into ecstasy as to put our mind and ourselves in God. Let us be driven by them, if we have first done what is in our power. For if through moral philosophy the forces of our passions have by a fitting agreement become so intent on harmony that they can sing together in undisturbed concord, and if through dialectic our reason has moved progressively in a rhythmical measure, then we shall be stirred by the frenzy of the Muses and drink the heavenly harmony with our inmost hearing. Thereupon Bacchus, the leader of the Muses, by showing in his mysteries, that is, in the visible signs of nature, the invisible things of God to us who study philosophy, will intoxicate us with the fulness of God's house, in which, if we prove faithful, like Moses, hallowed theology shall come and inspire us with a doubled frenzy. For, exalted to her lofty height, we shall measure therefrom all things that are and shall be and have been in indivisible eternity; and, admiring their original beauty, like the seers of Phoebus, we shall become her own winged lovers. And at last, roused by ineffable love as by a sting, like burning Seraphim rapt from ourselves, full of divine power we shall no longer be ourselves but shall become He Himself Who made us.

If anyone investigates the holy names of Apollo [as contained in Greek mystical writings], their meanings and hidden mysteries, these amply show that that god is no less a philosopher than a seer; but, since Ammonius [an Alexandrian Neo-Platonist of the sixth century] has sufficiently examined this subject, there is no reason why I should now treat it otherwise. But, Fathers, three Delphic pre-

cepts may suggest themselves to your minds, which are very necessary to those who are to go into the most sacred and revered temple,
not of the false but of the true Apollo, who lights every soul as it
enters this world. You will see that they give us no other advice
than that we should with all our strength embrace this threefold
philosophy which is the concern of our present debate. For the
saying μηδὲν ἄγαν that is, "Nothing too much," prescribes a standard
and rule for all the virtues through the doctrine of the Mean, with
which moral philosophy duly deals. Then the saying γνῶθι σεαυτόν
that is, "Know thyself," urges and encourages us to the investigation
of all nature, of which the nature of man is both the connecting
link and, so to speak, the "mixed bowl." For he who knows himself
in himself knows all things, as Zoroaster first wrote, and then Plato
in his *Alcibiades*. When we are finally lighted in this knowledge by
natural philosophy, and nearest to God are uttering the theological
greeting, εἶ that is, "Thou art," we shall likewise in bliss be ad-
dressing the true Apollo on intimate terms.

Let us also consult the wise Pythagoras, especially wise in that he
never deemed himself worthy the name of a wise man. He will first
enjoin us not to sit on a bushel, that is, not by unoccupied sloth
to lose our rational faculty, by which the soul measures, judges,
and considers all things; but we must direct and stimulate it un-
remittingly by the discipline and rule of dialectic. Then he will
point out to us two things particularly to beware of: that we should
not make water facing the sun or cut our nails while offering sacri-
fice. But after we have, through the agency of moral philosophy,
both voided the lax desires of our too abundant pleasures and
pared away like nail-cuttings the sharp corners of anger and the
stings of wrath, only then may we begin to take part in the holy
rites, that is, the mysteries of Bacchus we have mentioned, and to
be free for our contemplation, whose father and leader the Sun is
rightly named. Finally, Pythagoras will enjoin us to feed the cock,
that is, to feast the divine part of our soul on the knowledge of
things divine as if on substantial food and heavenly ambrosia. This
is the cock at whose sight the lion, that is, all earthly power, trembles
and is filled with awe. This is that cock to whom, we read in *Job*,
intelligence was given. When this cock crows, erring man comes to
his senses. This cock in the twilight of morning daily sings with

the morning stars as they praise God. The dying Socrates, when he hoped to join the divinity of his spirit with the divinity of a greater world, said that he owed this cock to Aesculapius, that is, to the physician of souls, now that he had passed beyond all danger of illness.

Let us review also the records of the Chaldeans, and we shall see (if they are to be trusted) the road to felicity laid open to mortals through the same sciences. His Chaldaean interpreters write that it was a saying of Zoroaster that the soul is winged and that, when the wings drop off, she falls headlong into the body; and then, after her wings have grown again sufficiently, she flies back to heaven. When his followers asked him in what manner they could obtain souls winged with well-feathered wings, he replied: "Refresh ye your wings in the waters of life." Again when they asked where they should seek those waters, he answered them thus by a parable (as was the custom of the man):

> God's paradise is laved and watered by four rivers, from whose same source ye may draw the waters of your salvation. The name of that in the north is Pischon, which meaneth the right. The name of that in the west is Dichon, which signifieth expiation. The name of that in the east is Chiddikel, which expresseth light, and of that in the south, Perath, which we may interpret as piety.

Turn your attention, Fathers, to the diligent consideration of what these doctrines of Zoroaster mean. Surely nothing else than that we should wash away the uncleanness from our eyes by moral science as if by the western waves; that we should align their keen vision toward the right by the rule of dialectic as if by the northern line; that we should then accustom them to endure in the contemplation of nature the still feeble light of truth as if it were the first rays of the rising sun, so that at last, through the agency of theological piety and the most holy worship of God, we may like heavenly eagles boldly endure the most brilliant splendor of the meridian sun. These are, perhaps, those ideas proper to morning, midday, and evening first sung by David and given a broader interpretation by Augustine. This is that noonday light which incites the Seraphs to their goal and equally sheds light on the Cherubs.

This is that country toward which Abraham, our father of old, was ever journeying. This is that place where, as the doctrines of Cabalists and Moors have handed down to posterity, there is no room for unclean spirits. And, if it is right to bring into the open anything at all of the occult mysteries, even in the guise of a riddle, since a sudden fall from heaven has condemned the head of man to dizziness, and, in the words of Jeremiah, death has come in through our windows and smitten our vitals and our heart, [then] let us summon Raphael, celestial physician, that he may set us free by moral philosophy and by dialectic as though by wholesome drugs. Then, when we are restored to health, Gabriel, "the strength of God," shall abide in us, leading us through the miracles of nature and showing us on every side the merit and the might of God. He will at last consign us to the high priest Michael, who will distinguish those who have completed their term in the service of philosophy with the holy office of theology as if with a crown of precious stones.

These, reverend Fathers, are the considerations that have not only inspired but compelled me to the study of philosophy. I should certainly not set them forth were I not answering those who are wont to condemn the study of philosophy, especially among men of rank or even of a mediocre station in life. For this whole study of philosophy has now (and it is the misfortune of our age) come to despite and contumely rather than to honor and glory. Thus this deadly and monstrous conviction has come to pervade the minds of well-nigh all—that philosophy either must be studied not at all or by few persons, as if it were absolutely nothing to have clearly ascertained, before our eyes and before our hands, the causes of things, the ways of nature, the plan of the universe, the purposes of God, and the mysteries of heaven and earth; unless one may obtain some favor, or make money for one's self. Rather, it has come to the point where none is now deemed wise, alas, save those who make the study of wisdom a mercenary profession, and where it is possible to see the chaste Pallas, who was sent among men as the gift of the gods, hooted, hissed, and whistled off the stage; and not having anyone to love or to befriend her, unless by selling herself, as it were, she repays into the treasury of her "lover" even the ill-gained money received as the poor price of her tarnished virginity.

I speak all these accusations (not without the deepest grief and indignation) not against the princes of this time but against the philosophers, who both believe and openly declare that there should be no study of philosophy for the reason that no fee and no compensation have been fixed for philosophers, just as if they did not show by this one sign that they are no philosophers, that since their whole life is set either on profit or on ambition they do not embrace the very discovery of truth for its own sake. I shall grant myself this and blush not at all to praise myself to this extent that I have never studied philosophy for any other reason than that I might be a philosopher; and that I have neither hoped for any pay from my studies, from my labors by lamplight, nor sought any other reward than the cultivation of my mind and the knowledge of the truth I have ever longed for above all things. I have always been so desirous, so enamored of this, that I have relinquished all interest in affairs private and public and given myself over entirely to leisure for contemplation, from which no disparagements of those who hate me, no curses of the enemies of wisdom, have been able in the past or will be able in the future to discourage me. Philosophy herself has taught me to rely on my own conscience rather than on the opinions of others, and always to take thought not so much that people may speak no evil of me, as, rather, that I myself may neither say nor do aught that is evil.

For my part, reverend Fathers, I was not unaware that this very disputation of mine would be as grateful and pleasing to you who favor all good sciences, and have been willing to honor it with your most august presence, as it would be offensive and annoying to many others. And I know there is no lack of those who have heretofore condemned my project, and who condemn it at present on a number of grounds. Enterprises that are well and conscientiously directed toward virtue have been wont to find no fewer—not to say more—detractors than those that are wickedly and falsely directed toward vice. There are, indeed, those who do not approve of this whole method of disputation and of this institution of publicly debating on learning, maintaining that it tends rather to the parade of talent and the display of erudition than to the increase of learning. There are those who do not indeed disapprove this kind of practice, but who in no wise approve it in me because I, born I admit but twenty-four years ago, should have dared at my age to offer a disputation concerning the lofty mysteries of Christian theology, the highest topics of philosophy and unfamiliar branches of knowledge, in so famous a city, before so great an assembly of very learned men, in the presence of the apostolic senate. Others, who give me leave to offer this disputation, are unwilling to allow me to debate nine hundred theses, and misrepresent it as being a work as unnecessary and as ostentatious as it is beyond my powers. I would have yielded to their objections and given in immediately if the philosophy I profess had so instructed me; and I should not now be answering them, even with philosophy as my preceptress, if I believed that this debate between us had been undertaken for the purpose of quarreling and scolding. Therefore, let the whole intention to disparage and to exasperate depart from our minds, and malice also, which Plato writes is ever absent from the heavenly choir. Let us in friendly wise try both questions: whether I am to debate and whether I am to debate about this great number of theses.

First, as to those who revile this custom of debating in public I shall certainly not say a great deal, since this crime, if it is held a crime, is shared with me not only by all of you, excellent doctors, who have rather frequently engaged in this office not without the highest praise and glory, but also by Plato, also by Aristotle, and also by the most worthy philosophers of every age. For them it was certain that, for the attainment of the knowledge of truth they were always seeking for themselves, nothing is better than to attend as often as possible the exercise of debate. For just as bodily energy is strengthened by gymnastic exercise, so beyond doubt in this wrestling-place of letters, as it were, energy of mind becomes far stronger and more vigorous. And I could not believe, either that the poets, by the arms of Pallas which they sang, or that the Hebrews, when they called the sword the symbol of wise men, were indicating to us anything else than that such honorable contests are surely a necessary way of attaining wisdom. For this reason it is, perchance, that the Chaldaeans desired in the horoscope of one who was to be a philosopher that Mars should be to Mercury in the trinal [i.e. triple; presumably has astrological significance] aspect, as much as to say, "If these assemblies, these disputations, should be given up, all philosophy would become sluggish and drowsy."

But truly with those who say I am unequal to this commission, my method of defense is more difficult. For if I say that I am equal to it, it seems that I shall take on myself the reproach of being immodest and of thinking too well of myself, and, if I admit that I am not equal to it, the reproach of being imprudent and thoughtless. See into what straits I have fallen, in what a position I am placed, since I cannot without blame promise about myself what I cannot then fail to fulfill without blame. Perhaps I could refer to that saying of Job: "The spirit is in all men," and be told with Timothy, "Let no man despise thy youth." But out of my own conscience I shall with more truth say this: that there is nothing either great or extraordinary about me. I do not deny that I am, if you will, studious and eager for the good sciences, but nevertheless I neither assume nor arrogate to myself the title of learned. However great the burden I may have taken on my shoulders, therefore, it was not because I was not perfectly aware of my own want of strength but because I knew that it is a distinction of contests of this kind, that is, literary ones, that there is a profit in being defeated. Whence it is that even the most feeble are by right able and bound not only not to decline but even more to court them, seeing that he who yields receives no injury but a benefit from the victor, in that through him he returns home even richer, that is, wiser and better equipped for future contests. Inspired by this hope, I, who am but a feeble soldier, have feared not at all to wage so burdensome a war with the strongest and most vigorous men of all. Whether this action be ill considered or not may be judged from the outcome of the battle and not from my age.

It remains in the third place to answer those who take offense at the great number of my propositions, as if the weight of these lay on their shoulders, and as if the burden, such as it is, were not rather to be borne by me alone. It is surely unbecoming and beyond measure captious to wish to set bounds to another's effort and, as Cicero says, to desire moderation in a matter which is the better as it is on a larger scale. In so great a venture it was necessary for me either to give complete satisfaction or to fail utterly. Should I succeed, I do not see why what is laudable to do in an affair of ten theses should be deemed culpable to have done also in an affair of nine hundred. Should I fail, they will have the wherewithal to accuse me if they hate me and to forgive me if they love me. For the failure of a young man with but slender talent and little learning in so grave and so great a matter will be more deserving of pardon than of blame. Nay, according to the poet: "If strength fails, there shall surely be praise for daring; and to have wished for great things is enough." And if many in our time, in imitation of Gorgias of Leontini, have been wont, not without praise, to propose debates not concerning nine hundred questions only, but also concerning all questions in all branches of knowledge, why should I not be allowed, and that without criticism, to discuss questions admittedly numerous but at least fixed and limited? Yet they say it is unnecessary and ostentatious. I contend that this enterprise of mine is in no way superfluous but necessary indeed; and if they will ponder with me the purpose of studying philosophy, they must, even against their wills, admit that it is plainly needful. Those who have devoted themselves to any one of the schools of philosophy, favoring, for instance, Thomas or Scotus, who are now most in fashion, are, to be sure, quite capable of making trial of their particular doctrines in the discussion of but a few questions. I, on the other hand, have so prepared myself that, pledged to the doctrines of no man, I have ranged through all the masters of philosophy, investigated all books, and come to know all schools. Therefore, since I had to speak of them all in order that, as champion of the beliefs of one, I might not seem fettered to it and appear to place less value on the rest, even while proposing a few theses concerning individual schools I could not help proposing a great number concerning all the schools together. And let no man condemn me for coming as a friend whithersoever the tempest bear me. For it was a custom observed by all the ancients in studying every kind of writer to pass over none of the learned works they were able to read, and especially by Aristotle, who for this reason was called by Plato ἀναγνώστης, that is, "reader." And surely it is the part of a narrow mind to have confined itself within a single Porch or Academy. Nor can one rightly choose what suits one's self from all of them who has not first come to be familiar with them all. Consider, in addition, that there is in each school something distinctive that is not common to the others. . . .

FRANCESCO MATARAZZO

Francesco Matarazzo was born about 1443 in Deruta, a small town near Perugia. He acquired the rudiments of a classical education, and spent a great part of his adult life as a professor, first at Ferrara, and later at Vicenza, Venice, and Perugia. His interest in Greek literature, and possibly in the profitable market for manuscripts, inspired him to travel to Greece in 1472. There, according to his own account, he learned the language well. During the 1490s he settled in Perugia, of which he became chancellor in 1503. Until 1513 he remained active in the city's diplomatic affairs. He died in 1518.

As it has come down to us, Matarazzo's *Chronicle of the City of Perugia,* covering the period 1492-1503, is an eyewitness account of the events it narrates and the people it describes. The author was a zealously patriotic Perugian, and an enthusiastic supporter of the city's ruling family, the Baglioni. Though he occasionally expresses shock at the ruthlessness and savagery of their rule, he undeniably idealizes their characters and achievements to the limits of credibility. His style is lively enough, but he seems rustic and provincial in comparison with the other humanists included here. Matarazzo is therefore a good example of a traditional civic chronicler of the late fifteenth century. His work interests us as documentation, not as literature.

The following selection is characteristic of Matarazzo's narrative style, though it deals with topics of broader interest than the history of his beloved Perugia. It first describes the activities of the papal court of Alexander VI centering around

113

the forthcoming third marriage of his daughter, Lucretia Borgia, to Alfonso I, Duke of Ferrara, in 1502. It then presents an interesting verbal portrait of Morgante Baglione, the Lord of Perugia, on the occasion of his death by poisoning. Here are some of the more lurid aspects of the period, as seen by a gifted observer. (From *Chronicle of the City of Perugia*, by Francesco Matarazzo. Translated by Edward S. Morgan. New York: E. P. Dutton & Co., Inc., 1905, pp. 208-14, 216-22. Reprinted by permission of J. M. Dent & Sons, Ltd.)

From Matarazzo's *Chronicle*

The Chief Pontiff, Alexander VI [Rodrigo Borgia (1431-1503), a Spaniard who became Pope in 1492,] had a daughter, Lucretia by name. Her he separated from her husband and made her divorce him. He then gave her to another husband, who in turn died at the hand of the Duke of Candia, brother to the said Lady Lucretia, with whom, though she was his sister, he had adulterous intercourse. [Both were children of Borgia's favorite mistress, Vanozza dei Cattani.] Then, to leave much untold, he gave her [as] wife to a third husband, the son of the Marques of Ferrara, which Marques, because he had some doubt as to the security of his dominion, allied himself in this way with the Holy Father in order that he should not overthrow his rule, as he had done to many states throughout the whole of Italy. He gave his daughter as a dowry a hundred thousand florins and made public promise besides to bestow on her other great wealth. And when the time came that she should be married the Pope had made for her a pair of slippers that cost more than three thousand ducats; and from this you may consider how much was the worth of her other jewels and magnificences. And so great was the estate and wealth that she brought to her husband that, as people say, she brought to him up to the value of three hundred thousand florins. After this fashion did it to the Pope seem fit to obey the commandment of the Church—to marry women and virgins.

And to do honor to the departure of this lady, Rome was for many days given over to festival and games. And at last, the evening of the day before her departure, the Pope gave a great supper to which he bade those whom he thought fit. Many ladies came to it, and among others his beloved daughter. And when they had supped the Pope called for the players, and after his guests had been mightily diverted he led the Lady Lucretia his daughter to the stable, in which there were many mares and stallions, and they were greatly amused with what they saw. Then, as if this were not enough, they returned to the reception hall, and there he had the lights put out; then the men and women left their clothes and had diversion. This it was that gave eternal fame to the Holy Shepherd; this his performance was indeed kindly and honorable! How did he, with his divine wisdom, forestall the desires of those who came to that joyous festival! But perchance what I tell you is but a weariness to your ears, and the more so should any of you not believe my story. Yet I would not venture to say anything of it if I thought that it was a lie. But inasmuch as the thing was noised abroad, and because my testimony and witness are the people of Rome, aye and of Italy, therefore have I written. Perchance God will let my conscience prick me for that I write such things of the Chief Pontiff, yet that my work may be complete I wrote what you have read above.

Thereafter when she was to set out on her journey a palanquin [a covered litter, usually carried by four or six men] was provided built of wood covered with cloth and lined inside with gold and drapery exceeding rich; for the bearing of which two hundred men were ordered. There was room inside for several people so that the bride Lucretia could travel with greater comfort when she was weary of riding. Thus she set out for Ferrara, at one time riding, at another in the palanquin, or whatever other fitter name you will give to her carriage, after she had taken leave of her dear father and of her brother. There rode in her train many gentlemen and prelates, and of horses fifteen hundred and more; and this is very truth. And the cavalcade was a sore trouble and expense to the towns and villages through which it passed; for the expense was great, so great as to be beyond belief. For each town subject to the Church must needs pass her on with all honor to the next. . . . So to this Lady Lucretia great honor was done throughout her progress. For her Ladyship bore the great banner of all loose women, and was the leader of her fellows. So much concerning her, though there would be much more to tell; but to tell of her has become to me mere weariness, therefore here I make stay and will relate no more.

Now Pope Alexander had throughout his reign, by means lawful and unlawful, collected and stored up money beyond tale, and great treasure, yet his boundless and insatiable appetite, and the great hunger which his avarice provoked constrained him ever to pile up treasure. So his Sacred Majesty determined to become a merchant, and brought a great quantity of grain from Sicily to Rome. Then His Holiness made proclamation that no one besides himself should dare to sell corn in Rome, and caused so great dearth and famine in Rome that no bread was found in the city, so that the poor folk were brought to their death for hunger, and by this means he managed to gain fifty carlins for each measure of wheat. Howbeit fortune did not speed him, but rather wrecked several of his ships laden with corn; not that he therefore lost any of his capital, but his profits were less than they would otherwise have been.

In the city of Pisa, as people say, there was a treasonable understanding contrived by the Pope, who designed to reduce that city, as you may readily believe, to the rule of his outland [i.e., foreign] Duke [Caesar Borgia]. So he gave it out that he intended to go to Piombino and see the lordship that he had acquired for his boy, and thence to travel to Romagna, visiting the towns on his way. And under that color he proposed to enter Pisa and get possession of it. Now from the day that that city had revolted from the lordship of Florence it had passed all its time in woe, and it was seldom that an army did not lie round it. Howbeit by the time that the Pope reached Piombino the great treachery had been discovered, so that it was to no purpose that he should have gone any further. Meanwhile in Rome provision was made to deliver the citizens from the great dearth that the merchant Pope Alexander VI had caused. After this he returned, for his purpose had come to naught.

And after the Pope had done these things, because of his desire to promote his outland son to great glory and power and wealth, another device came into his mind—to make him creditor of the Roman Church. And so he did, and made him appear as creditor of the said Church for the sum of two hundred thousand ducats. And in order that he might have the better security he gave him in

[Margin notes, handwritten:]

Alexander took $ lawfully & unlawfully. Controlled corn market & created famine in Rome

Wanted to give Pisa to his son, Duke, but couldn't +

The Pope makes the Duke Creditor of the Church. Pays him & gives him a Castle in Rome pawn the Castle of St. Angelo which is in Rome. As this thing has been told to me, so I tell it to you.

Nor with all this was Pope Alexander content, but determined to put into act his design with regard to the lordship of Camerino. Indeed he had oftimes before been urged to make war against the Lord of Camerino, and that by certain nephews of that lord, because they had by him been exiled, and they claimed that lordship as their own. So the Pope was fully determined to take his lordship from him and give it to his outland son. To accomplish this design he looked for aid to the high and mighty Baglioni, who still had engraved on their hearts the cruel injury that the Lord of Camerino had done them when he devised that great betrayal which had brought so low the high and mighty house of the Baglioni; wherefore willingly and more than willingly they made tender of all their resources for this purpose. And that this might be done orderly they called out a levy of all the city, ward by ward, and each ward had its own banner with the arms and colors that were theirs of old; and on each one was the splendid silver griffin. Never had there been seen a more magnificent show in our city, for every man bore a lance colored after the color of the banner of his ward. In every street and every square you saw citizens in the harness of soldiers; and for these few days no other business was attended to in the city. . . . Thus cavalry and infantry were equipped beyond all count, to assault the Lord of Camerino and beat him to the ground, and requite him for his wicked deeds.

About this time, that is in June 1502, there was a plot in Arezzo, and the town revolted from Florence; and they sent for aid to the two captains Vitelozzo and Giovan' Paolo who joined them, and at once marched against the Florentines harrying the Upper Valdarno, and forcing the villages there to surrender to them; and because all the substance of the towns and villages lay out in the open, that is the crops ready for the sickle, every man and every township made terms with them, that they might not suffer loss of the harvest; and thus those captains quickly subdued a large tract. On hearing this the commonwealth of Florence determined to provide against the injury done, and hired His Highness Morgante Baglione to serve them, allowing him pay for a hundred and thirty lances and promising him beside to appoint him in short time Captain-General, with the command of other two hundred mercenaries. . . . Now when the Duke of Valentia [Caesar Borgia] heard this, he at once sent for His Highness Morgante and urged him to become his captain and promised to increase his pay. But for all his promises the high and mighty Morgante would not accept his pay, and refused to break faith with the high and mighty commonwealth of Florence; which thing was a great grief to the Duke of Valentia.

Now His Highness Morgante Baglione, as he marched toward the Florentine territory, must needs halt for some days at Borghetto above Lake Trasimene. For Cortona had already revolted from the Florentines and with it all the surrounding country. But His Highness Giovan' Paolo Baglione, being captain of the Sienese, seized on the pass of Valiano and closed that passage into the Florentine territory; so that His Highness Morgante must needs apply to the commonwealth of Siena for leave of passage. And he got leave to march through with thirty or forty horsemen a day, but no more. So the army was kept so long in that bad climate that many of the soldiers fell ill and among others His Highness. Nevertheless they continued their advance toward Florence. And when the two captains Giovan' Paolo and Vitelozzo heard this, fearing that His Highness Morgante Baglione might effect a junction with the other Florentine forces, they sent at once to the commonwealth of Siena asking that he should not be allowed passage. And this was granted them, so that His Highness Morgante was not able to reach the Florentine territory. Meanwhile His Highness sickened daily more and more of the sore disease that was on him, yet he remained there many days making light of his serious illness, if he could by any means find way of passage. . . .

His Highness Morgante Baglione was encamped, as I have told you, on the bank of the lake, endeavoring to get across into Tuscany, nor did he know how grievous was the disease that was ever more wasting his strength. Though weak, as if death were knocking at the door, he did not recognize the insidious nature of the sickness that sapped his strength, but thought that he suffered only from the malign and pestilential air. So he moved and came to Pacciano where he tried with doctors and drugs to heal him of his wasting disease, but all was in vain, and it seemed that the end had come and he must die. Then was it seen that envy at least was not yet dead; for one of his servants gave him a poison against which no antidote was of any avail. But His Highness, when he felt that death had hold of him, sent for his brother Messer Gentile and, clasping his hand, set forth to him at length what it behooved him to do for his personal safety and that of the state. His hour was now come; short time remained ere he must lay aside this mortal coil. His tongue with which he had above all others pleaded the cause of the people of Perugia cleaved to the roof of his mouth. No more word could he utter, for death said him nay. Around all stood wondering at the body that lay before them. All wept, relations and soldiers, the death of that high lord.

Hardly had the breath left him when there came a messenger from Florence bringing promise of a more important command and yet greater distinction and renown; and this added to the bitter grief of his brothers and friends for the death of that glorious lord. And when they heard of his death the Signory of Florence regretted it profoundly, for they had already determined among themselves to give him the Staff of Command and make him their Captain-General. For never had a man been found loyal like unto him.

Methinks that it is not in these pages of mine that I can relate how this honorable lord, worthy to be had in everlasting remembrance, passed from this life; at such length were it fitting to tell of his death in prose or in verse, [in] Latin or in the vulgar tongue; with stately phrase and dignified recounting all his glorious deeds, whose fame shall never pass away, but give unfading luster to the ancient city of his birth. So as any lengthier narrative of mine would but manifest the more its own inadequacy, I will merely say that on the seventeenth of the month of July 1502, a victim of jealousy, this noble and illustrious captain died, slain by traitors and their most cruel poison; and by his death our city was widowed of a hero that brought her great honor, and of a much-loved son. Not a man there was but bewailed the death of him who bequeathed to his city and to every citizen glory and renown that shall never fade. And it was remarked that when he died exactly two years and two days had passed since his father and brothers were cut off in the pride of their honorable lives. In his death our hero was in every way honored, but above all by the untold tears that were shed, and by the infinite mourning of citizens and of soldiers, and of all who had ever known him. His body was brought to Perugia to the Church of San Francesco and there buried with ample ritual beside his ancestors.

Here I would fain take leave of him, and cease to speak of one whose cruel death so moves to grief and wrath, but though no words of mine could portray and honor him as becomes his worth, yet it is seemly that I should say something more concerning him. And since you, who hear or read my tale, may perhaps wonder at my too fond words, I answer and say that Nature and Justice demand that the brave man be honored and glorified before and after death, for good report lives for ever: and it is the more seemly that he should be honored by me that write these words, in that he is to us of Perugia an eternal glory and renown; fame and repute he brings to this ancient city of his birth, wherefore let men never weary to tell the praise and honor of him, and of every hero, as beseems the splendor of his courage. I say therefore that never did Nature so richly endow any man with all high gifts of soul as she did this honorable lord, and this shall appear from my short description of him. His form was well knit and lordly; taller he was than any other man, and his graceful limbs were so admirably proportioned that men commonly said that never in Italy had been seen a man more fair to look on, with arms or without, riding or afoot. When My Lord came into the Piazza all citizens followed in his train, and the craftsmen left their work to gaze upon his Lordship. And when My Lord went forth with the army all soldiers thronged round his tent door to see his Lordship, even as at the coming of the King of France, and such was his presence that he outshone all other lords and made them seem as naught. And Nature that had endowed him with so admirable frame and form appointed his birth in an ancient and glorious city, above all others haughty and apt for war, in which had never failed a race of honorable men to win her name and fame in the art military; wherefore she made him citizen of this our city of Perugia, for which he won so great honor and glory. And for greater assurance of renown he was born of that ancient and noble family the House of the Baglioni, beyond compare more than any other family of Italy fit for arms and battle, fruit in very truth of the loins of Mars. These were from of old, as I learn, masters of the art of war. And well did he follow in the footsteps of his lineage and relations. Abundant honor did he bring to Italy, especially to lovely Tuscany, to his ancient city of Perugia, and to the distant founder of his race. To Germany also he brought honor, whence, as the elders among us say, that family first came, by the glorious deeds that he did, though of these I here say naught, for I touch but briefly on the story of his life. Moreover he was born to be lord of castles and of towns. Yet another excellent gift Nature bestowed on him, in that she endowed him with a mind and character that made him loved of all that knew him, and won for him the admiration even of his enemies, and not a man was there of his but would have died for him. Just he was and dignified beyond all men, and his conversation sincere and seemly; greed of wealth never had any hold on him, who was generous and free-handed and governed his life with splendor and magnificence. He kept and maintained permanently in his court a hundred and six-teen at table, without taking count of the friends and visitors who were from day to day entertained by himself and his relations. For if any man of any account visited our city he was honorably en-treated by the high and mighty House of the Baglioni. Nothing I say here of the heavy expense of clothing for themselves and their relations; for as yet they were still draped in mournful robes of black for the dismal death of his father and brothers—tables, drap-ery, furniture, soldiers all black. Nor shall I tell of his other sump-tuosities, horses, mules, dogs, falcons, jesters, singers, outlandish animals, befitting the state of a noble lord. Never would he have listened to any one asking him to sell his influence for money; and the man who had suggested such a thing to him he would have treated as a mortal enemy. Each year his expenditure so outran his income as to me seems incredible. Above all providence, that had bestowed on him all these gifts of high rank and noble character, and other excellences too of which I cannot tell you, thought well to set on his head a crown which should add luster to all his other qualities, a crown that shone with a light more splendid than the sun's; that crown was the crown of Justice; for in his noble heart Justice was enshrined beside all his other virtues. He was a man utterly just and fair, and so immovably determined to give each man his due, that all the gold that ever was coined would not have made him turn aside, or wrest justice in the estimation of one poor scruple. A man more upright was never seen in our city of Perugia, who for a thousand ducats would not have told a single lie. More just he was than even Numa Pompilius, whom, because he was so just, the Romans made their king. And he had so many other excellent qualities that I will not tell them, for so my tale would be too tedious. Finally the encomium of his sad death, or rather I should say his noble life, was written by Francesco Matarazzo. This I pass in silence. And here I make an end, and pass to another subject, merely adding in conclusion that while he held sway and government, he was never blamed for any thought or act, save perhaps that he was too scrupulous in administering justice, and that more in affairs in which he was himself concerned than in the affairs of strangers. A thing wonderful and hardly to be believed.

℀ NICCOLÒ MACHIAVELLI

Niccolò Machiavelli (1469-1527) was born to an impoverished family of the lesser Florentine aristocracy. He was trained mainly in notarial and secretarial skills, which served to qualify him for the minor positions that he occupied within the Republican government of Florence between 1498 and 1512, the year of his imprisonment, alleged torture, and eventual exile. During his period of public service he was often called upon to participate in diplomatic missions to foreign as well as Italian courts, and his reports to the Florentine *signoria* are mines of information on the regions in which he traveled, the people he observed, and the problems that it fell to him to analyze and interpret.

Upon his enforced retirement to his modest villa near San Casciano—a retirement from which he was never permitted to emerge—Machiavelli began to commit to paper the insights on political behavior which he had been developing over years of historical studies and close personal observation. He was keenly aware of the inadequacies of traditional political treatises, with their conventional moral exhortations. He realized that in order to govern effectively, a ruler needed to know how men do in fact behave, not only how they ought to behave, so that he could use appropriate means to achieve his objectives. Only in the last hundred years has it become generally understood that Machiavelli was not the cynical, wicked "Old Nick" caricatured by the Elizabethan playwrights, but rather a decent and brilliant, if perhaps one-sided, man who was whole-heartedly committed to trying to understand the ruthless and complicated world he knew.

The selection which follows is taken from *The Prince,* and represents only a brief portion of that short treatise. *The*

123

Prince cannot be properly understood without reference to Machiavelli's desire to please the Medici and return to active political life, his belief that Italy was in need of a strongman, and his extreme patriotic fervor. Thus, his concern is to instruct the "man on horseback" on how to gain and maintain power, so as to restore Italy to the grandeur that he, as a good humanist historian, saw in its past. Analytical and persuasive elements are both at work in *The Prince;* it is, as these excerpts show, a theoretical treatise as well as a tract for the times. (From *The Prince and the Discourses,* by Niccolò Machiavelli. Ricci translation, revised by E. R. P. Vincent. London: Oxford University Press, 1949. Copyright by Oxford University Press. Reprinted by permission of the publishers.)

From *The Prince*
Chapter XV
Of the Things for Which Men, and Especially Princes, Are Praised or Blamed

It now remains to be seen what are the methods and rules for a prince as regards his subjects and friends. And as I know that many have written of this, I fear that my writing about it may be deemed presumptuous, differing as I do, especially in this matter, from the opinions of others. But my intention being to write something of use to those who understand, it appears to me more proper to go to the real truth of the matter than to its imagination; and many have imagined republics and principalities which have never been seen or known to exist in reality; for how we live is so far removed from how we ought to live, that he who abandons what is done for what ought to be done, will rather learn to bring about his own ruin than his preservation. A man who wishes to make a profession of goodness in everything must necessarily come to grief among so many who are not good. Therefore it is necessary for a prince, who wishes to maintain himself, to learn how not to be good, and to use this knowledge and not use it, according to the necessity of the case.

Leaving on one side, then, those things which concern only an imaginary prince, and speaking of those that are real, I state that

all men, and especially princes, who are placed at a greater height,
are reputed for certain qualities which bring them either praise or
blame. Thus one is considered liberal, another *misero* or miserly
(using a Tuscan term, seeing that *avaro* with us still means one who
is rapaciously acquisitive and *misero* one who makes grudging use
of his own); one a free giver, another rapacious; one cruel, another
merciful; one a breaker of his word, another trustworthy; one effem-
inate and pusillanimous, another fierce and high-spirited; one humane, another haughty; one lascivious, another chaste; one frank,
another astute; one hard, another easy; one serious, another frivolous; one religious, another an unbeliever, and so on. I know that
every one will admit that it would be highly praiseworthy in a
prince to possess all the above-named qualities that are reputed
good, but as they cannot all be possessed or observed, human conditions not permitting of it, it is necessary that he should be prudent enough to avoid the scandal of those vices which would lose
him the state, and guard himself if possible against those which
will not lose it him, but if not able to, he can indulge them with
less scruple. And yet he must not mind incurring the scandal of
those vices, without which it would be difficult to save the state,
for if one considers well, it will be found that some things which
seem virtues would, if followed, lead to one's ruin, and some others
which appear vices result in one's greater security and wellbeing.

Chapter XVII
Of Cruelty and Clemency, and Whether It Is Better to Be Loved or Feared

Proceeding to the other qualities before named, I say
that every prince must desire to be considered merciful and not
cruel. He must, however, take care not to misuse this mercifulness.
Caesar Borgia was considered cruel, but his cruelty had brought
order to the Romagna, united it, and reduced it to peace and
fealty. If this is considered well, it will be seen that he was really
much more merciful than the Florentine people, who, to avoid the
name of cruelty, allowed Pistoia [an outlying town northwest of
Florence] to be destroyed. A prince, therefore, must not mind in-

curring the charge of cruelty for the purpose of keeping his subjects united and faithful; for, with a very few examples, he will be more merciful than those who, from excess of tenderness, allow disorders to arise, from whence spring bloodshed and rapine; for these as a rule injure the whole community, while the executions carried out by the prince injure only individuals. And of all princes, it is impossible for a new prince to escape the reputation of cruelty, new states being always full of dangers. Wherefore Virgil through the mouth of Dido says:

> Res dura, et regni novitas me talia cogunt
> Moliri, et late fines custode tueri.

[The newness of the kingdom and hard reality compel me to undertake such things, and to guard the borders with a lookout on all sides. (*Aeneid* I, 563-64)]

Nevertheless, he must be cautious in believing and acting, and must not be afraid of his own shadow, and must proceed in a temperate manner with prudence and humanity, so that too much confidence does not render him incautious, and too much diffidence does not render him intolerant.

From this arises the question whether it is better to be loved more than feared, or feared more than loved. The reply is, that one ought to be both feared and loved, but as it is difficult for the two to go together, it is much safer to be feared than loved, if one of the two has to be wanting. For it may be said of men in general that they are ungrateful, voluble dissemblers, anxious to avoid danger, and covetous of gain; as long as you benefit them, they are entirely yours; they offer you their blood, their goods, their life, and their children, as I have before said, when the necessity is remote; but when it approaches, they revolt. And the prince who has relied solely on their words, without making other preparations, is ruined; for the friendship which is gained by purchase and not through grandeur and nobility of spirit is bought but not secured, and at a pinch is not to be expended in your service. And men have less scruple in offending one who makes himself loved than one who makes himself feared; for love is held by a chain of obligation which, men being selfish, is broken whenever it serves their purpose;

but fear is maintained by a dread of punishment which never fails.

Still, a prince should make himself feared in such a way that if he does not gain love, he at any rate avoids hatred for fear and the absence of hatred may well go together, and will be always attained by one who abstains from interfering with the property of his citizens and subjects or with their women. And when he is obliged to take the life of anyone, let him do so when there is a proper justification and manifest reason for it; but above all he must abstain from taking the property of others, for men forget more easily the death of their father than the loss of their patrimony. Then also pretexts for seizing property are never wanting, and one who begins to live by rapine will always find some reason for taking the goods of others, whereas causes for taking life are rarer and more fleeting.

But when the prince is with his army and has a large number of soldiers under his control, then it is extremely necessary that he should not mind being thought cruel; for without this reputation he could not keep an army united or disposed to any duty. Among the noteworthy actions of Hannibal is numbered this, that although he had an enormous army, composed of men of all nations and fighting in foreign countries, there never arose any dissension either among them or against the prince, either in good fortune or in bad. This could not be due to anything but his inhuman cruelty, which together with his infinite other virtues, made him always venerated and terrible in the sight of his soldiers, and without it his other virtues would not have sufficed to produce that effect. Thoughtless writers admire on the one hand his actions, and on the other blame the principal cause of them.

And that it is true that his other virtues would not have sufficed may be seen from the case of Scipio (famous not only in regard to his own times, but all times of which memory remains), whose armies rebelled against him in Spain, which arose from nothing but his excessive kindness, which allowed more license to the soldiers than was consonant with military discipline. He was reproached with this in the Senate by Fabius Maximus, who called him a corrupter of the Roman militia. Locri having been destroyed by one of Scipio's officers was not revenged by him, nor was the insolence of that officer punished, simply by reason of his easy nature; so much so, that someone wishing to excuse him in the

Senate, said that there were many men who knew rather how not to err, than how to correct the errors of others. This disposition would in time have tarnished the fame and glory of Scipio had he persevered in it under the empire, but living under the rule of the Senate this harmful quality was not only concealed but became a glory to him.

I conclude, therefore, with regard to being feared and loved, that men love at their own free will, but fear at the will of the prince, and that a wise prince must rely on what is in his power and not on what is in the power of others, and he must only contrive to avoid incurring hatred, as has been explained.

Chapter XVIII
In What Way Princes Must Keep Faith

How laudable it is for a prince to keep good faith and live with integrity, and not with astuteness, everyone knows. Still the experience of our times shows those princes to have done great things who have had little regard for good faith, and have been able by astuteness to confuse men's brains, and who have ultimately overcome those who have made loyalty their foundation.

You must know, then, that there are two methods of fighting, the one by law, the other by force: the first method is that of men, the second of beasts; but as the first method is often insufficient, one must have recourse to the second. It is therefore necessary for a prince to know well how to use both the beast and the man. This was covertly taught to rulers by ancient writers, who relate how Achilles and many others of those ancient princes were given to Chiron the centaur to be brought up and educated under his discipline. The parable of this semi-animal, semi-human teacher is meant to indicate that a prince must know how to use both natures, and that the one without the other is not durable.

A prince being thus obliged to know well how to act as a beast must imitate the fox and the lion, for the lion cannot protect himself from traps, and the fox cannot defend himself from wolves. One must therefore be a fox to recognize traps, and a lion to frighten wolves. Those that wish to be only lions do not understand this. Therefore, a prudent ruler ought not to keep faith when by so doing it would be against his interest, and when the reasons which made him bind himself no longer exist. If men were all good, this precept would not be a good one; but as they are bad, and would not observe their faith with you, so you are not bound to keep faith with them. Nor have legitimate grounds ever failed a prince who wished to show colorable excuse for the non-fulfillment of his promise. Of this one could furnish an infinite number of modern examples, and show how many times peace has been broken, and how many promises rendered worthless, by the faithlessness of princes, and those that have been best able to imitate the fox have succeeded best. But it is necessary to be able to disguise this character well, and to be a great feigner and dissembler; and men are so simple and so ready to obey present necessities, that one who deceives will always find those who allow themselves to be deceived.

I will only mention one modern instance. [Pope] Alexander VI [1] did nothing else but deceive men, he thought of nothing else, and found the occasion for it; no man was ever more able to give assurances, or affirmed things with stronger oaths, and no man observed them less; however, he always succeeded in his deceptions, as he well knew this aspect of things.

It is not, therefore, necessary for a prince to have all the above-named qualities, but it is very necessary to seem to have them. I would even be bold to say that to possess them and always to observe them is dangerous, but to appear to possess them is useful. Thus it is well to seem merciful, faithful, humane, sincere, religious, and also to be so; but you must have the mind so disposed that when it is needful to be otherwise you may be able to change to the opposite qualities. And it must be understood that a prince, and especially a new prince, cannot observe all those things which are considered good in men, being often obliged, in order to maintain the state, to act against faith, against charity, against humanity, and against religion. And, therefore, he must have a mind disposed to

---

[1] For another view of Pope Alexander VI, see the previous selection, by Francesco Matarazzo. [ED.]

adapt itself according to the wind, and as the variations of fortune dictate, and, as I said before, not deviate from what is good, if possible, but be able to do evil if constrained.

A prince must take great care that nothing goes out of his mouth which is not full of the above-named five qualities, and, to see and hear him, he should seem to be all mercy, faith, integrity, humanity, and religion. And nothing is more necessary than to seem to have this last quality, for men in general judge more by the eyes than by the hands, for everyone can see, but very few have to feel. Everybody sees what you appear to be, few feel what you are, and those few will not dare to oppose themselves to the many, who have the majesty of the state to defend them; and in the actions of men, and especially of princes, from which there is no appeal, the end justifies the means. Let a prince therefore aim at conquering and maintaining the state, and the means will always be judged honorable and praised by everyone, for the vulgar is always taken by appearances and the issue of the event; and the world consists only of the vulgar, and the few who are not vulgar are isolated when the many have a rallying point in the prince. A certain prince of the present time, whom it is well not to name [Ferdinand of Aragon], never does anything but preach peace and good faith, but he is really a great enemy to both, and either of them, had he observed them, would have lost him state or reputation on many occasions.

Chapter XXV
How Much Fortune Can Do in Human Affairs and How It May Be Opposed

It is not unknown to me how many have been and are of opinion that worldly events are so governed by fortune and by God that men cannot by their prudence change them, and that on the contrary there is no remedy whatever, and for this they may judge it to be useless to toil much about them, but let things be ruled by chance. This opinion has been more held in our day, from the great changes that have been seen, and are daily seen, beyond every human conjecture. When I think about them, at times I am partly inclined to share this opinion. Nevertheless, that our free will may not be altogether extinguished, I think it may be true that fortune is the ruler of half our actions, but that she allows the other half or thereabouts to be governed by us. I would compare her to an impetuous river that, when turbulent, inundates the plains, casts down trees and buildings, removes earth from this side and places it on the other; every one flees before it, and everything yields to its fury without being able to oppose it; and yet though it is of such a kind, still, when it is quiet men can make provision against it by dikes and banks, so that when it rises it will either go into a canal or its rush will not be so wild and dangerous. So it is with fortune, which shows her power where no measures have been taken to resist her, and directs her fury where she knows that no dikes or barriers have been made to hold her. And if you regard Italy, which has been the seat of these changes, and [which] has given the impulse to them, you will see her to be a country without dikes or banks of any kind. If she had been protected by proper measures, like Germany, Spain, and France, this inundation would not have caused the great changes that it has, or would not have happened at all.

This must suffice as regards opposition to fortune in general. But limiting myself more to particular cases, I would point out how one sees a certain prince today fortunate and tomorrow ruined, without seeing that he has changed in character or otherwise. I believe this arises in the first place from the causes that we have already discussed at length; that is to say, because the prince who bases himself entirely on fortune is ruined when fortune changes. I also believe that he is happy whose mode of procedure accords with the needs of the times, and similarly he is unfortunate whose mode of procedure is opposed to the times. For one sees that men in those things which lead them to the aim that each one has in view, namely, glory and riches, proceed in various ways; one with circumspection, another with impetuosity, one by violence, another by cunning, one with patience, another with the reverse; and each by these diverse ways may arrive at his aim. One sees also two cautious men, one of whom succeeds in his designs, and the other not, and in the same way two men succeed equally by different methods, one being cautious, the other impetuous, which arises only from the nature of the times, which does or does not conform to their method of procedure. From this it results, as I have said, that two men, acting differently, attain the same effect, and of two others acting in the same way, one attains his goal and not the other. On this depend also the changes in prosperity, for if it happens that time and circumstances are favorable to one who acts with caution and prudence he will be successful, but if time and circumstances change he will be ruined, because he does not change his mode of procedure. No man is found so prudent as to be able to adapt himself to this, either because he cannot deviate from that to which his nature disposes him, or else because having always prospered by walking in one path, he cannot persuade himself that it is well to leave it; and therefore the cautious man, when it is time to act suddenly, does not know how to do so and is consequently ruined; for if one could change one's nature with time and circumstances, fortune would never change.

Pope Julius II [the "warrior pope," who reigned from 1503 to 1513] acted impetuously in everything he did and found the times and conditions so in conformity with that mode of procedure that he always obtained a good result. Consider the first war that he made against Bologna while Messer Giovanni Bentivogli [ruler of that city] was still living. The Venetians were not pleased with it, neither was the King of Spain; France was conferring with him over the enterprise, notwithstanding which, owing to his fierce and impetuous disposition, he engaged personally in the expedition. This move caused both Spain and the Venetians to halt and hesitate, the latter through fear, the former through the desire to recover the entire kingdom of Naples. On the other hand, he engaged with him the King of France, because seeing him make this move and desiring his friendship in order to put down the Venetians, that king judged that he could not refuse him his troops without manifest injury. Thus Julius by his impetuous move achieved what no other pontiff with the utmost human prudence would have succeeded in doing, because, if he had waited till all arrangements had been made and everything settled before leaving Rome, as any other pontiff would have done, it would never have succeeded. For the King of France would have found a thousand excuses, and the others would have inspired him with a thousand fears. I will omit his other actions, which were all of this kind and which all suc-

ceeded well, and the shortness of his life did not suffer him to experience the contrary, for had times followed in which it was necessary to act with caution, his ruin would have resulted, for he would
never have deviated from these methods to which his nature disposed him.

I conclude then that fortune varying and men remaining fixed
in their ways, they are successful so long as these ways conform to
circumstances, but when they are opposed then they are unsuccessful. I certainly think that it is better to be impetuous than cautious,
for fortune is a woman, and it is necessary, if you wish to master
her, to conquer her by force; and it can be seen that she lets herself be overcome by the bold rather than by those who proceed
coldly. And therefore, like a woman, she is always a friend to the
young, because they are less cautious, fiercer, and master her with
greater audacity.

The importance of fortune

Chapter XXVI
Exhortation to Liberate Italy
from the Barbarians

Having now considered all the things we have spoken of,
and thought within myself whether at present the time was not
propitious in Italy for a new prince, and if there was not a state of
things which offered an opportunity to a prudent and capable man
to introduce a new system that would do honor to himself and good
to the mass of the people, it seems to me that so many things con-
cur to favor a new ruler that I do not know of any time more fitting
for such an enterprise. And if, as I said, it was necessary in order
that the power of Moses should be displayed that the people of
Israel should be slaves in Egypt, and to give scope for the greatness
and courage of Cyrus that the Persians should be oppressed by the
Medes, and to illustrate the preeminence of Theseus that the
Athenians should be dispersed, so at the present time, in order that
the might of an Italian genius might be recognized, it was necessary
that Italy should be reduced to her present condition, and that she
should be more enslaved than the Hebrews, more oppressed than
the Persians, and more scattered than the Athenians; without a

head, without order, beaten, despoiled, lacerated, and overrun, and that she should have suffered ruin of every kind.

And although before now a gleam of hope has appeared which gave hope that some individual might be appointed by God for her redemption, yet at the highest summit of his career he was thrown aside by fortune, so that now, almost lifeless, she awaits one who may heal her wounds and put a stop to the pillaging of Lombardy, to the rapacity and extortion in the Kingdom of Naples and in Tuscany, and cure her of those sores which have long been festering. Behold how she prays God to send someone to redeem her from this barbarous cruelty and insolence. Behold her ready and willing to follow any standard if only there be someone to raise it. There is nothing now she can hope for but that your illustrious house may place itself at the head of this redemption, being by its power and fortune so exalted, and being favored by God and the Church, of which it is now the ruler. Nor will this be very difficult, if you call to mind the actions and lives of the men I have named. And although those men were rare and marvelous, they were nonetheless men, and each of them had less opportunity than the present, for their enterprise was not juster than this, nor easier, nor was God more their friend than He is yours. Here is a just cause; *"iustum enim est bellum quibus necessarium, et pia arma ubi nulla nisi in armis spes est."* [That war is just which is necessary, and those arms are pious where there is no hope save in arms.] Here is the greatest willingness, nor can there be great difficulty where there is great willingness, provided that the measures are adopted of those whom I have set before you as examples. Beside this, unexampled wonders have been seen here performed by God, the sea has been opened, a cloud has shown you the road, the rock has given forth water, manna has rained, and everything has contributed to your greatness, the remainder must be done by you. God will not do everything, in order not to deprive us of free will and the portion of the glory that falls to our lot.

It is no marvel that none of the before-mentioned Italians have done that which it is to be hoped your illustrious house may do; and if in so many revolutions in Italy and so many warlike operations, it always seems as if military capacity were extinct, this is because the ancient methods were not good, and no one has arisen who knew how to discover new ones. Nothing does so much honor to a newly risen man than the new laws and measures which he introduces. These things, when they are well based and have greatness in them, render him revered and admired, and there is not lacking scope in Italy for the introduction of every kind of new organization. Here there is great virtue in the members, if it were not wanting in the heads. Look how in duels and in contests of a few the Italians are superior in strength, dexterity, and intelligence. But when it comes to armies they make a poor show; which proceeds entirely from the weakness of the leaders, for those that know are not obeyed, and everyone thinks that he knows, there being hitherto nobody who has raised himself so high both by valour and fortune as to make the others yield. Hence it comes about that for so long a time, in all the wars waged during the last twenty years, whenever there has been an entirely Italian army it has always been a failure, as witness first Taro, then Alexandria, Capua, Genoa, Vaila, Bologna, and Mestri.

If your illustrious house, therefore, wishes to follow those great men who redeemed their countries, it is before all things necessary, as the true foundation of every undertaking, to provide yourself with your own forces, for you cannot have more faithful, or truer and better soldiers. And although each one of them may be good, they will united become even better when they see themselves commanded by their prince, and honored and favored by him. It is therefore necessary to prepare such forces in order to be able with Italian prowess to defend the country from foreigners. And although both the Swiss and Spanish infantry are deemed terrible, nonetheless they each have their defects, so that a third method of array might not only oppose them, but be confident of overcoming them. For the Spaniards cannot sustain the attack of cavalry, and the Swiss have to fear infantry which meets them with resolution equal to their own. From which it has resulted, as will be seen by experience, that the Spaniards cannot sustain the attack of French cavalry, and the Swiss are overthrown by Spanish infantry. And although a complete example of the latter has not been seen, yet an instance was furnished in the battle of Ravenna, where the Spanish infantry attacked the German battalions, which are organized in the same way as the Swiss. The Spaniards, through their bodily agility and aided by their bucklers, had entered between and under their pikes and were in a position to attack them safely without the Germans being able to defend themselves; and if the cavalry had not charged them they would have utterly destroyed them. Knowing therefore the defects of both these kinds of infantry, a third kind can be created which can resist cavalry and need not fear infantry, and this will be done by the choice of arms and a new organization. And these are the things which, when newly introduced, give reputation and grandeur to a new prince.

This opportunity must not, therefore, be allowed to pass, so that Italy may at length find her liberator. I cannot express the love with which he would be received in all those provinces which have suffered under these foreign invasions, with what thirst for vengeance, with what steadfast faith, with what love, with what grateful tears. What doors would be closed against him? What people would refuse him obedience? What envy could oppose him? What Italian would withhold allegiance? This barbarous domination stinks in the nostrils of everyone. May your illustrious house therefore assume this task with that courage and those hopes which are inspired by a just cause, so that under its banner our fatherland may be raised up, and under its auspices be verified that saying of Petrarch:

> Valour against fell wrath
> Will take up arms; and be the combat quickly sped!
> For, sure, the ancient worth,
> That in Italians stirs the heart, is not yet dead.

ℤ PIETRO BEMBO

Pietro Bembo was born in 1470, to one of the most distinguished Venetian families. Educated in the humanist tradition of Venice, with its special emphasis on Hellenic studies, he became a member of the learned circle that formed about the great printer Aldus Manutius in the 1490s. As a result of his father's activity as a Venetian diplomat, and of his high social position, Bembo was able to enjoy long stays in some of the most culturally active courts of Italy—Ferrara and Urbino, and later the Rome of Pope Leo X. In later life, after years of scholarly and literary activity, he was made a Cardinal. He died in 1547.

Bembo's remarkable ability to combine the active and contemplative lives is worth noting. His talents as a courtier would alone have made him famous, since he emerges as the most serious spokesman in Castiglione's *Courtier* (see selection reprinted below). He had many love affairs, including one with Lucretia Borgia, the wife of Alfonso d'Este, of the ruling house of Ferrara. He was also a noted historian of Venice, an arbiter of Italian literary style, and one of the most accomplished lyric poets of the sixteenth century.

Gli Asolani, a series of three dialogues on love first published in 1505, was written at intervals between 1494 and 1504. An immediate success, it was reprinted and re-edited frequently throughout the century, and also became popular in Spanish and French translations. Several views of love are presented throughout the work, and they reflect classical, naturalistic, courtly, and Platonic traditions. In the selection that follows, taken from the concluding section of the work, the meaning of perfect love is revealed. One of the discutants claims that, while wandering in a grove on a mountaintop near

Asolo (a town in Northern Italy where the dialogues take place, and whence their title), he came upon a bearded, white-haired man who proclaimed these truths. The Platonic elements here are readily identifiable, though they are not presented with philosophical rigor. Most of them are ideas about love, taken from the *Symposium.* Thus, the document is characteristic of much of the courtly and literary Platonic love theory that originated on a much higher level in the works of Marsilio Ficino, and which enjoyed a broad and deep influence on the literature of the late Renaissance. As this selection opens, Lavinello, the speaker in this dialogue, is quoting the words of the bearded old man to the courtiers assembled at Asolo. (From *Gli Asolani,* by Pietro Bembo. Translated by Rudolf B. Gottfried. Bloomington, Ind.: Indiana University Press, 1954, pp. 180-95. Copyright 1954 by Indiana University Press. Reprinted by permission of the publisher.)

From *Gli Asolani*

" 'Indeed, my son, if you would like to lift the world's dark veil aside in order to learn wisdom from gazing on the truth, you will find in the end that all the desires you esteem the most are only childish vanity. To omit those loves which are compact of misery, as Perottino's lovers and he himself can fully illustrate, what stability or rectitude or satisfaction can the others give that we should seek or prize them so excessively as Gismondo urged that we should do? [Perottino and Gismondo are previous participants in the dialogue.] I cannot see, indeed, how all these mortal charms with which sight, hearing, and the other senses nourish the mind, allowing them to enter and re-enter it a thousand times by means of thought—I cannot see how they avail us when they little by little overmaster us with pleasure so that we think of nothing else and, having lowered our eyes to worthless things, remain no longer true to ourselves, but change at last from men to beasts, as if we had taken the enchanted draft of Circe; nor can I understand how these charms can delight us so fully, even assuming that it is not a false delight, when they were never found nor shall be found so fully in one object that an observer might be gratified with every part and when they are rather few than tolerably free from harm.

" 'After every brief affair, moreover, they disappear in some little fever that we suffer, or at best, time bears them all away: youth, beauty, pleasure, graceful movements, tender words, songs, music, dancing, banquets, games, and all the other joys of love. They cannot fail to torture those who yearn for them, and all the more as the delights with which such lovers let themselves be haltered are the greater. If age does not rid them of these desires, what can be more wretched than to taint senility with childish wishes and animate weak, palsied limbs with callow thoughts? And if age does remove them, how foolish to love youthful things with so much ardor that one should fail to love his own maturity, or should believe that something in which the better part of life takes no delight or use is both more useful and delightful than all else? For the better part of our life, my son, is surely that in which our better part, namely the soul, is free from bondage to the appetites, and rules the worser part, the body, with temperance; in which reason guides the senses, which in the heat of youth will never hear its voice but blunder turbulently here and there at will. Concerning this, I, who have been a young man too, as you are now, can give you ample proof; and when I remember the things which at that time I was accustomed to desire and praise the most, they seem more paltry to me now than one who is well recovered finds the wishes which possessed him in the height of fever, wishes of which he now makes sport, knowing how far he wandered then from knowledge and good taste.

" 'It may be said therefore that old age is the health and youth the illness of our lives, the truth of which will strike you when you reach my years, if you cannot already understand it. To return, however, to your companion who in his discourse has exalted the many joys of lovers to the heavens, let us say only that the least of them are attended with a thousand discomforts; but when, even amid his most consummate pleasures, does he not sigh for something more? or when does that conformity of wills, that community of thought about their lot, that lifelong harmony occur between two lovers? For there is no man who does not have some disagreement with himself each day, sometimes of such a sort that if one could leave himself as two can leave each other, many would do so, taking another mind and body.

" 'To come to your loves also, Lavinello: I would praise them indeed and partly enter into your view if they made you desire some more useful object than the one they set before you, and if they pleased you not so much for themselves as because an understanding of them can bring us to a more perfect and less fallible condition. For virtuous love is not merely desire of beauty, as you believe, but desire of true beauty, which is not of that human and mortal kind which fades, but is immortal and divine; and yet these beauties that you praise may lift us to it, provided we regard them in the proper way. In that case what can be said in praise of them which does not fall beside the mark since men enamored of their charms leave human life behind, like gods? For those men are gods, my son, who as divinities scorn mortal things and as mortals aspire to things divine; who advise, discuss, foresee, take thought about eternity; who move and rule and moderate the body which is given them, just as the other gods dispose of things assigned to their control.

" 'And yet what beauty found among us can be so pleasant and entire, what fine proportion of the parts in some human receptacle, what harmonious conformity, that it could ever fill or satisfy our hearts completely? O Lavinello, Lavinello, you are not what this external form reveals, and other men likewise are not what they may outwardly appear; the soul of each is what he is, and not the body which is there for any finger to point out. Our souls are not of such a quality that they are able to conform and satisfy themselves with any beauty found down here. If you could put all of them there are before your mind and let it choose among them and correct at will whatever seemed amiss in any part, you would not satisfy it in the end, nor would you be any happier with earthly pleasures you had gathered far and wide than you are wont to be with those you now enjoy. Souls, being immortal, can never be contented with a mortal thing.

" 'But as all the stars draw light from the sun, all beauties which exist outside of the divine, eternal beauty are derived from it; and when our minds perceive these secondary beauties, they are pleased and gladly study them as likenesses and sparks of it, but they are never wholly satisfied with them because they yearn for that divine, eternal loveliness which they remember and for which they are ever secretly spurred on to search. Just as when a hungry man is overcome by sleep, he cannot satisfy his appetite by dreaming that he eats, since his hunger requires the food itself and not its likeness, so while we seek true beauty and true pleasure, which are elsewhere, we do not feed but only fool the soul by pursuing their mere shadows in these corporeal beauties and these mundane pleasures. This we must take care to avoid, in order that our good genius may not grow angry with us and abandon us to our evil one when he sees that we bear more love to the surface of one little face and to these wretched and deceitful charms than to that mighty splendor whose ray is called the sun or to its true and everlasting beauties. This life of ours is even a kind of sleep; and just as those who lie down late at night with the thought of rising early on the morrow will dream of getting up and thus while still asleep will rise and begin to draw their mantles on, so in our very dreams we strive to find, not the mere likeness of food or these vain and shadowy delights, but food itself and firm and pure contentment, and they begin to nourish us while we are still asleep, so that when we are awakened, we may give pleasure to the Queen of the Fortunate Isles.—But perhaps you have not already heard of this queen?'

" 'No, father, I don't seem to remember her, nor do I understand the pleasure of which you speak.'

" 'Then you will hear about it now,' the holy man pursued. 'Among their most esoteric memories, the ancients who were wise in sacred things held that on those islands which I have called Fortunate there was a queen of surpassing beauty, adorned with costly garments and ever young, who still remained a virgin, not wishing for a husband, but well contented to be loved and sought. And to those who loved her more she gave a greater reward; to the others one suitable to their affection. But she tested all of them as follows:

" 'When each had come before her, as she had had them summoned one by one, she touched them with a wand and sent them off; and as soon as they had left the palace, they fell asleep and remained asleep until she had them wakened. When they returned to her presence once more, each had written on his forehead an exact description of his dreams which she instantly read. And those whose dreams she saw to have dealt only with hunting, fishing, horses, forests, and wild beasts she drove from her, commanding them to spend their waking hours among the creatures of which they made companions in their sleep; for she said that if they had loved her, they would have dreamed of her at least once and that since they had never done so, she would have them live with their beasts. Of those others whose dreams had evidently been concerned with trade or governing their families and communities or similar things, yet little with the queen herself, she appointed one to be a merchant, one a citizen, one an elder in his city, weighing them down with heavy thoughts and taking no more care for them than they for her. But those who had dreamed they were with her she kept about her court to talk to her amid music, songs, and rounds of endless pleasure, one nearer and one further off according as they had spent a larger or a smaller portion of their dreams with her.

" 'But perhaps I am delaying you too much now, Lavinello, when you must wish or need rather to return to your companions than to hear me any longer. Moreover, it might hurt you to delay your departure till the sun is higher, for it already fills the sky with heat and is still gathering its strength.'

" 'Neither wish nor need in any way compels me to return, my father,' I hastened to put in; 'and if talking is not inconvenient for you, sure[ly] I know of nothing which I have ever done more willingly than listen to your words. And don't worry about the height of the sun, for I have only to walk downhill, which would be easy at any hour.'

" 'Old men are not wont to find talking inconvenient,' he replied, 'for it is an amusement peculiar to age; nor can anything be inconvenient to me which brings you pleasure. So let us continue.

" 'To Perottino and Gismondo, then, I would say, my son, that if they did not wish to be sent among the beasts when they woke up, they should seek some better dream than theirs is now. And as for you, Lavinello, don't assume that the queen will hold you dear when you have dreamed of her so little, wasting your sleep among these unprofitable vanities rather than employing it for some really useful purpose. Know, in fine, that your love is not virtuous.

Granted that it is not evil like those which are mingled with bestial desires; still it falls short of virtue because it does not draw you toward an immortal object but holds you midway between the extremes of desire where it is not safe to remain, for on a slope it is easier to slide into the depths than to clamber to the summit. And is not one who trusts to the pleasures of some sense, although he does not intend to fall into evil ways, likely, at least at times, to be ensnared? for sense is full of deceits, making the same things appear to be sometimes good and sometimes evil, sometimes fair and sometimes foul, sometimes pleasing and sometimes spiteful. Furthermore, how can any desire be virtuous which rests on sensuous pleasures as it were on water, pleasures degrading those who have them, tormenting those who lack them, and all as fugitive as the brief moment? Nor can the fine, distinguished phrases with which such lovers speak of it change the thing itself; for even if thought perpetuate these delights, how much better it would be not to have our heavenly, immortal minds than, having them, to clog and, as it were, to bury them in earthly thoughts! They were not given us that we should nourish them on mortal poison, but rather on restorative ambrosia, whose flavor never torments or degrades, being always dear and precious. And this can happen only if we turn our souls back to that God who gave them to us.

" 'You will do so, my son, if you will listen to me and consider that He has spread Himself throughout this sacred temple which we call the earth, and in His marvelous wisdom made it circular, revolving on itself, and of itself both needy and replete. He girt it in with many spheres of purest substance which ever turn around it, the greatest moving contrariwise to all the rest; on one of them He set the countless stars which shine on every side, and to each of the other spheres assigned a star to hold, commanding all of them to draw their light from that great splendor which guides them on their courses, divides the night from day, produces time, and begets and governs all things born. He made these luminaries perform their cycles on fixed paths, completing them and, when completed, beginning them once more, each in a less or greater period. And under all of these He placed the purer element of fire and filled all that remained, from there to us, with air. And in the middle, or lowest part, He fixed the earth, as if it were the ridge of the temple, and surrounded it with the waters, which are a lighter element than earth, though heavier than air, which in its turn is heavier than fire.

" 'Here you will be delighted to determine how their four kinds of qualities are mingled through these four parts and how they simultaneously agree and disagree; delighted to study the phases of the changing moon, the labors of the sun, the varied courses of the wandering stars and of those which do not wander, and by considering the causes and the functions of them all to lead your mind around the heavens. Conversing with nature as it were, you will learn how brief and paltry are the things we love on earth, when the greatest length of this human life can hardly fill two days of one celestial year and the least star of that infinite multitude is greater than this solid sphere which we so proudly call the earth and of which, in turn, the place that we inhabit is only a microscopic particle. Here, moreover, everything is weak and sickly, what with winds, rain, ice, snow, cold, heat, fevers, colics, vomits, and other such diseases which have assailed us ever since the opening of Pandora's splendid box exposed us to these harms; while there all things are strong and reach a state so perfect that neither death nor age nor any lack can overcome them.

" 'But your delight and wonder will be even greater, Lavinello, if you can pass from these heavens which you see to those which are unseen and contemplate the things which are actually there, ascending from one to another until you raise your desires to that beauty which surpasses them and every other beauty. For those who are used to gazing with the eyes of the soul no less than of the body have no doubt that beyond this sensible, material world of which I have spoken, as everyone speaks more often of what he sees, there lies another world which is neither material nor evident to sense, but completely separate from this, and pure; a world which turns around this one and is both sought and found by it, wholly divided from it and wholly abiding in each part of it; a world divine, intelligent, and full of light, itself as much beyond itself in size and virtue as it draws nearer to its Final Cause.

" 'That world contains all that we have in this, but things as much more excellent than these as the heavenly are better than the earthly here. For just as this world has its earth, so that has its green earth too which puts forth plants and feeds its animals and has its sea to mingle with, its ambient air, its fire, its moon, its sun, its stars, its other spheres. But there the grass is never brown, the plants are never withered, the creatures never die, the seas are never rough, the air is never dark, the fire never parches, nor must its heavens and their bodies turn continually. That world has no need of any change, for neither summer nor winter, nor yesterday nor tomorrow, nor near nor far, nor large nor small confines it; but it rests contented with its state, having achieved the highest self-sufficiency and happiness, and being big with it, gives birth to this very world you see before you. And if we think that there can be no other than the one we see, we are like a man who having spent his days from birth deep in the abysm of the sea, would for that reason be unable to imagine by himself that there were other things above the water, nor would believe that elsewhere he might find branches fairer than seaweed, or meadows more delightful than the sands, or animals more gay than fish, or habitations of another kind than stony caverns, or other elements than earth and water.

" 'But were he to rise into our region and see the vivid greenery of fields and woods and hills; the variety of creatures, some born to feed us and some to aid us; the cities, temples, houses standing here; the many arts and ways of life; the purity of the air; the brilliance of the sun which, by scattering its light through heaven, makes the day and kindles the stars with which the darkness of the night is splendid; and all the other so various and endless beauties of the world—he would understand how mistaken he had been and would not wish his old life back at any price. So we wretches who are assigned to live upon this filthy ball of earth, seeing the air and the birds who cleave it, feel the same wonder as that with which we see only in part. Beside all these, however, we have many more things to admire than our ocean man would find on earth, things marvelous and dear whose what or how our poor intelligence can never grasp. Yet were some god to carry us up there and show them to us, Lavinello, only those would seem real to us, and the life led there the true one, and all that is here but a shadow or picture of their existence; and gazing down from that serene height on other men among these shadows here below, we would call ourselves wretched and pity them, nor ever willingly return to such a life.

" 'But what can I say to you, Lavinello? You are young, and in youth, apparently, such thoughts do not take root; or if they do, they for the most part grow poorly, as if they had been planted in the shade. Nevertheless, if they should enter your youthful mind when you are charmed down here by the dim light of two eyes already full of death, what must you make of those eternal splendors which are so true, so pure, so mild? And if the sound of some tongue delights you which caused you to weep only a little earlier and which will be silent soon forever, how precious must you find the discourse and the harmony made by the heavenly choruses in unison? And when you take such satisfaction from thinking of some silly woman's doings, one like so many here, what satisfaction do you think your soul would take if it were to purify itself of these delusions and in its innocence to reach those shining forms, to gaze with growing concentration on the great works of that Lord who rules above, and to bring its chaste affections and desires as an offering to Him?

" 'This pleasure is too great, my son, for anyone to understand who has not proved it, and none can prove it who cares a straw for other pleasures. For the sun cannot be endured by such mole's eyes as those with which our souls, blindfolded by their longings, see; nay, even the most clearsighted does not reach that far. But some stranger, passing before the palace of a king, even though he cannot see or otherwise know that it belongs to a king, surmises that some great man must live there, since he sees it full of servants, and thinks him greater as those servants are more dignified and dressed more richly; in the same way, although we cannot see that mighty Lord at all, we can yet say that He must be a mighty lord since all the elements and all the heavens minister to Him and serve His majesty. Therefore, your friends will do wisely if they will henceforth court this Prince as they have wooed their ladies hitherto, and if remembering that they are in a temple, they will now dispose themselves to pray since they have had enough of vanities, and casting aside false, earthly, mortal love, will clothe themselves in that which is true, celestial, and immortal. And this it would be well for you to do likewise.

" 'For every good accompanies this heavenly desire, and every ill is far from it. There none encounter rivalries, suspicions, or jealousies since, however many love Him, many more may love Him also and enjoy their love as thoroughly as one alone would do; that infinite Godhead can satisfy us all and yet remain eternally the same. There none need fear treachery or harm or broken faith. Nothing unsuitable is sought, or granted, or desired. The body receives what is sufficient, as Cerberus is thrown a biscuit lest he bark; and the soul enjoys what it requires most. Nor is anyone forbidden to seek what he loves or denied the power to attain that delight to which his love impels him. Nor do men go by land and sea, or climb on walls or roofs, to find what they desire. Nor is there need of arms or messenger or escort; for God is all that each can see or wish. Neither anger nor scorn nor repentance nor change nor joy deceptive nor vain hope nor grief nor fear is found there. There neither chance nor fortune can prevail. There all is full of certainty, content, and happiness.

" 'And those things which other men love so much down here and to secure which we so often see the whole world thrown into confusion, the very streams run red with human blood, and even the ocean on occasion, as this wretched age of ours has often known and still knows, for that matter—empires and crowns and lordships, I mean—: these are no more sought by one of our celestial lovers than he who can have water from a pure wellspring, when he is thirsty will seek that of some turbid, marshy rivulet. If, on the other hand, poverty, exile, or oppression overtakes him, as one who dwells here sees befalling every day, he receives it with a smile, remembering that it makes little difference which cloth covers or land contains or wall encloses this body, and that the little love he bears such things does not deprive the mind of its wealth, its country, or its freedom. In brief, he neither welcomes happy circumstances with too much delight nor equally refuses to live out the bitter ones, but temperately endures them both as long as the Lord who gave them wills that he should linger here. And while other lovers fear death throughout their lives as something which will bring all their revels to an end, and make that journey, when they reach it, with melancholy and unwillingness, he goes there joyfully when he is called, believing he has changed a wretched inn for his own house that overflows with gladness and festivity. And what, if not an inn, can this life be called, which is rather a kind of death through which we journey, with all its grievances assailing us from every side so often, with all its constant partings from what we love the most, with all its deaths from day to day of those who are most dear to us, with all its other mishaps that every hour give us reason to weep, and these more often the more we think we ought to be enjoying peace and pleasure?

" 'You can tell how far this is true of your own case. To me indeed it seems a thousand years before I can unloose the wrapping of my flesh, and flying from this prison or deceitful inn, return to the place from which I came, and when the eyesight lost upon this journey is recovered, can see that indescribable beauty which I, thanks to its own beneficence, have loved so long already. And though I am an old man now, as you perceive, it holds me no less dear than it has always done, nor will deny me because I come before it in such a humble garb. Not that I shall go there in this form, any more than you will go in yours; for no one takes anything beside his loves from here. And if they are attached to these beauties here below, they torment us since they cannot rise upward but are fixed in the earth which bore them, just as we are now tormented by desires which cannot in the least be satisfied. If our loves are, on the other hand, celestial, they bring a marvelous contentment since we can reach them and enjoy them fully. Nay, furthermore, our future state is everlasting, Lavinello, and so we must believe that virtuous love is to be eternally enjoyed and that the other which is evil damns us to eternal grief.'

"When the holy man had said so much, he allowed me to depart, for it was time that I should do so." And with these words Lavinello brought his discourse to a close.

℀ BALDESAR
CASTIGLIONE

Castiglione was born in the duchy of Mantua in 1478, and died in 1529. After periods of residence at several other courts, he joined the service of the family of Montefeltro, the Dukes of Urbino. There he remained from 1504 to 1524, when he was appointed papal nuncio to Spain, and later, Bishop of Avila. An accomplished Latin and Italian stylist both in prose and verse, he was also a living model of the courtier's elegance of taste and grace of manner.

It is interesting to compare him with Machiavelli, whose life spanned most of the same period. Machiavelli was an unsuccessful courtier, a product of an essentially republican environment, a man whose interests and sensitivities were quite narrowly political. Contemporary portraits reveal him as small, thin, pale, with sharp features, a penetrating glance, a subtle, mobile expression. Castiglione spent most of his life in courtly societies, had been educated as a humanist, and embodied a considerable variety of talents and interests. Raphael has preserved him for us—his fine, composed features, his aristocratic carriage, his elegant attire. Machiavelli's prose is simple, terse, economical; Castiglione's is rhetorical, elaborate, literary. Machiavelli's writings reflect the chaos and confusion of Italian political and military affairs; Castiglione's reveal the refinement and charm of the Renaissance court.

The Book of the Courtier was finished by 1516, but did not appear in print until 1528. Though written as a conversation, or dialogue—a favorite form among the humanists—it came to be regarded as an almost canonical description of the Renaissance ideals of human personality. In the sixteenth and early seventeenth centuries in France and England, Castiglione's

149

picture of the perfect courtier provided a model for men of wealth and ambition. Many books of etiquette appeared in its wake, to lead men step by step from the real to the ideal. Two brief passages have been selected from this long and delightful work. They develop two of the most important qualities required in the courtier—proficiency in arms and excellence in letters. Here it is possible to see a direct relationship between the earlier educational theorists of the fifteenth century and the arbiter of courtly taste in the sophisticated little world of Urbino, where these conversations took place. The participants include celebrated noblemen, courtiers, humanists, and ladies. As this selection begins, Count Ludovico da Canossa is describing for the assembled group some qualities he believes a good courtier must have. (From *The Book of the Courtier,* by Baldesar Castiglione. Translated by Charles S. Singleton. Garden City, N.Y.: Doubleday & Company, Inc., 1959, pp. 32-39, 67-74. Copyright © 1959 by Charles S. Singleton and Edgar DeN. Mayhew. Reprinted by permission of Doubleday & Company, Inc.)

From *The Courtier*

BOOK I

"I hold that the principal and true profession of the Courtier must be that of arms which I wish him to exercise with vigor; and let him be known among the others as bold, energetic, and faithful to whomever he serves. And the repute of these good qualities will be earned by exercising them in every time and place, inasmuch as one may not ever fail therein without great blame. And, just as among women the name of purity, once stained, is never restored, so the reputation of a gentleman whose profession is arms, if ever in the least way he sullies himself through cowardice or other disgrace, always remains defiled before the world and covered with ignominy. Therefore, the more our Courtier excels in this art, the more will he merit praise; although I do not deem it necessary that he have the perfect knowledge of things and other qualities that befit a commander, for since this would launch us on too great a sea, we shall be satisfied, as we have said, if he have complete loyalty and an undaunted spirit, and be always seen to have them. For oftentimes men are known for their courage in small things rather than in great. And often in important perils and where there are many witnesses, some men are found who, although their hearts sink within them, still, spurred on by fear of shame or by the company of those present, press forward with eyes shut, as it were, and do their duty, God knows how; and in things of little importance and when they think they can avoid the risk of danger, they are glad to play safe. But those men who, even when they think they will not be observed or seen or recognized by anyone, show courage and are not careless of anything, however slight, for which they could be blamed, such have the quality of spirit we are seeking in our Courtier.

"However, we do not wish him to make a show of being so fierce that he is forever swaggering in his speech, declaring that he has wedded his cuirass, and glowering with such dour looks as we have often seen Berto [probably a buffoon] do; for to such as these one may rightly say what in polite society a worthy lady jestingly said to a certain man (whom I do not now wish to name) whom she sought to honor by inviting him to dance, and who not only declined this but would not listen to music or take any part in the other entertainments offered him, but kept saying that such trifles were not his business. And when finally the lady said to him: 'What then is your business?' he answered with a scowl: 'Fighting.' Whereupon the lady replied at once: 'I should think it a good thing, now that you are not away at war or engaged in fighting, for you to have yourself greased all over and stowed away in a closet along with all your battle harness, so that you won't grow any rustier than you already are'; and so, amid much laughter from those present, she ridiculed him in his stupid presumption. Therefore, let the man we are seeking be exceedingly fierce, harsh, and always among the first, wherever the enemy is; and in every other place, humane, modest, reserved, avoiding ostentation above all things as well as that impudent praise of himself by which a man always arouses hatred and disgust in all who hear him."

Then signor Gasparo replied: "As for me, I have known few men excellent in anything whatsoever who did not praise themselves;

and it seems to me that this can well be permitted them, because he who feels himself to be of some worth, and sees that his works are ignored, is indignant that his own worth should lie buried; and he must make it known to someone, in order not to be cheated of the honor that is the true reward of all virtuous toil. Thus, among the ancients, seldom does anyone of any worth refrain from praising himself. To be sure, those persons who are of no merit, and yet praise themselves, are insufferable; but we do not assume that our Courtier will be of that sort."

Then the Count said: "If you took notice, I blamed impudent and indiscriminate praise of one's self: and truly, as you say, one must not conceive a bad opinion of a worthy man who praises himself modestly; nay, one must take that as surer evidence than if it came from another's mouth. I do say that whoever does not fall into error in praising himself and does not cause annoyance or envy in the person who listens to him is indeed a discreet man and, besides the praises he gives himself, deserves praises from others; for that is a very difficult thing."

Then signor Gasparo said: "This you must teach us."

The Count answered: "Among the ancients there is no lack of those who have taught this; but, in my opinion, the whole art consists in saying things in such a way that they do not appear to be spoken to that end, but are so very apropos that one cannot help saying them; and to seem always to avoid praising one's self, yet do so; but not in the manner of those boasters who open their mouths and let their words come out haphazardly. As one of our friends the other day who, when he had had his thigh run through by a spear at Pisa, said that he thought a fly had stung him; and another who said that he did not keep a mirror in his room because when he was angry he became so fearful of countenance that if he were to see himself, he would frighten himself too much."

Everyone laughed at this, but Messer Cesare Gonzaga added: "What are you laughing at? Do you not know that Alexander the Great, upon hearing that in the opinion of one philosopher there were countless other worlds, began to weep, and when asked why, replied: 'Because I have not yet conquered one'—as if he felt able to conquer them all? Does that not seem to you a greater boast than that of the fly sting?"

Then said the Count: "And Alexander was a greater man than the one who spoke so. But truly one has to excuse excellent men when they presume much of themselves, because anyone who has great things to accomplish must have the daring to do those things, and confidence in himself. And let him not be abject and base, but modest rather in his words, making it clear that he presumes less of himself than he accomplishes, provided such presumption does not turn to rashness."

When the Count paused here briefly, Messer Bernardo Bibbiena said, laughing: "I remember you said before that this Courtier of ours should be naturally endowed with beauty of countenance and person, and with a grace that would make him lovable. Now this grace and beauty of countenance I do believe that I have myself, wherefore it happens that so many ladies, as you know, are ardently in love with me; but, as to the beauty of my person, I am rather doubtful, and especially as to these legs of mine which in truth do not seem to me as well disposed as I could wish; as to my chest and the rest, I am quite well enough satisfied. Now to determine a little more in detail what this beauty of body should be, so that I can extricate myself from doubt and put my mind at ease."

After some laughter at this, the Count added: "Certainly such grace of countenance you can truly be said to have; nor will I adduce any other example in order to make clear what that grace is; because we do see beyond any doubt that your aspect is very agreeable and pleasant to all, although the features of it are not very delicate: it has something manly about it, and yet is full of grace. And this is a quality found in many different types of faces. I would have our Courtier's face be such, not so soft and feminine as many attempt to have who not only curl their hair and pluck their eyebrows, but preen themselves in all those ways that the most wanton and dissolute women in the world adopt; and in walking, in posture, and in every act, appear so tender and languid that their limbs seem to be on the verge of falling apart; and utter their words so limply that it seems they are about to expire on the spot; and the more they find themselves in the company of men of rank, the more they make a show of such manners. These, since nature did not make them women as they clearly wish to appear and be, should be treated not as good women, but as public harlots, and driven not only from the courts of great lords but from the society of all noble men.

"Then, coming to bodily frame, I say it is enough that it be neither extremely small nor big, because either of these conditions causes a certain contemptuous wonder, and men of either sort are gazed at in much the same way that we gaze at monstrous things. And yet, if one must sin in one or the other of these two extremes, it is less bad to be on the small side than to be excessively big; because men who are so huge of body are often not only obtuse of spirit, but are also unfit for every agile exercise, which is something I very much desire in the Courtier. And hence I would have him well-built and shapely of limb, and would have him show strength and lightness and suppleness, and know all the bodily exercises that befit a warrior. And in this I judge it his first duty to know how to handle every kind of weapon, both on foot and on horse, and know the advantages of each kind; and be especially acquainted with those arms that are ordinarily used among gentlemen, because, apart from using them in war (where perhaps so many fine points are not necessary), there often arise differences between one gentleman and another, resulting in duels, and quite often those weapons are used which happen to be at hand. Hence, knowledge of them is a very safe thing. Nor am I one of those who say that skill is forgotten in the hour of need; for he who loses his skill at such times shows that out of fear he has already lost his heart and head.

"I deem it highly important, moreover, to know how to wrestle, because this frequently accompanies the use of weapons on foot. Then, both for his own sake and for his friends', he must understand the quarrels and differences that can arise, and must be alert to seize an advantage, and must show courage and prudence in all things. Nor should he be quick to enter into a fight, except insofar as his honor demands it of him; for, besides the great danger that an uncertain fate can bring, he who rushes into such things precipitately and without urgent cause deserves greatly to be censured, even though he should meet with success. But when he finds that he is so far involved that he cannot withdraw without reproach, he must be very deliberate both in the preliminaries to the duel and in the duel itself, and always show readiness and daring. Nor must he do as some who spend their time in wrangling and arguing over points of honor; and, when they have the choice of weapons, select those which neither cut nor prick, and arm themselves as if they were expecting to stand against cannonades; and, thinking it enough not to be defeated, stand always on the defensive and give ground to such a degree that they show extreme cowardice. And so they make themselves the laughingstock of children, like those two men from Ancona who fought at Perugia recently and made everyone laugh who saw them."

"And who were they?" asked signor Gaspar Pallavicino.

"Two cousins," replied Messer Cesare.

Then the Count said: "In their fighting they seemed true brothers." Then he went on: "Weapons are also often used in various exercises in time of peace, and gentlemen are seen in public spectacles before the people and before ladies and great lords. Therefore I wish our Courtier to be a perfect horseman in every kind of saddle; and, in addition to having a knowledge of horses and what pertains to riding, let him put every effort and diligence into outstripping others in everything a little, so that he may be always recognized as better than the rest. And even as we read that Alcibiades surpassed all those peoples among whom he lived, and each in the respect wherein it claimed greatest excellence, so would I have this Courtier of ours excel all others in what is the special profession of each. And as it is the peculiar excellence of the Italians to ride well with the rein, to manage wild horses especially with great skill, to tilt and joust, let him be among the best of the Italians in this. In tourneys, in holding a pass, in attacking a fortified position, let him be among the best of the French. In stick-throwing, bull-fighting, in casting spears and darts, let him be outstanding among the Spaniards. But, above all, let him temper his every action with a certain good judgment and grace, if he would deserve that universal favor which is so greatly prized.

"There are also other exercises which, although not immediately dependent upon arms, still have much in common therewith and demand much manly vigor; and chief among these is the hunt, it seems to me, because it has a certain resemblance to war. It is a true pastime for great lords, it befits a Courtier, and one understands why it was so much practiced among the ancients. He should also know how to swim, jump, run, throw stones; for, besides their usefulness in war, it is frequently necessary to show one's prowess in such things, whereby a good name is to be won, especially with the crowd (with whom one must reckon after all). Another noble exercise and most suitable for a man at court is the game of tennis which shows off the disposition of body, the quickness and litheness of every member, and all the qualities that are brought out by almost every other exercise. Nor do I deem vaulting on horseback to be less worthy, which, though it is tiring and difficult, serves more than anything else to make a man agile and dextrous; and besides its usefulness, if such agility is accompanied by grace, in my opinion it makes a finer show than any other.

"If, then, our Courtier is more than fairly expert in such exercises, I think he ought to put aside all others, such as vaulting on the ground, rope-walking, and the like, which smack of the juggler's trade and little befit a gentleman.

"But since one cannot always engage in such strenuous activities (moreover, persistence causes satiety, and drives away the admiration we have for rare things), we must always give variety to our lives by changing our activities. Hence, I would have our Courtier descend sometimes to quieter and more peaceful exercises. And, in order to escape envy and to enter agreeably into the company of others, let him do all that others do, yet never depart from comely conduct, but behave himself with that good judgment which will not allow him to engage in any folly; let him laugh, jest, banter, frolic, and dance, yet in such a manner as to show always that he is genial and discreet; and let him be full of grace in all that he does or says. . . ."

[The conversation now turns to other arts and skills. We rejoin it on the subject of right learning, a central concern of the Renaissance moralist.]

"But, besides goodness, for everyone the true and principal adornment of the mind is, I think, letters; although the French recognize only the nobility of arms and reckon all the rest as nought; and thus not only do they not esteem, but they abhor letters, and consider all men of letters to be very base; and they think that it is a great insult to call anyone a clerk."

Then the Magnifico Giuliano replied: "What you say is true; this error has prevailed among the French for a long time now. But if kind fate will have it that Monseigneur d'Angoulême [the future King Francis I, a renowned patron of the arts] succeed to the crown, as is hoped, then I think that just as the glory of arms flourishes and shines in France, so must that of letters flourish there also with the greatest splendor. Because, when I was at that court not so long ago, I saw this prince; and, besides the disposition of his body and the beauty of his countenance, he appeared to me to have in his aspect such greatness (yet joined with a certain gracious humanity) that the realm of France must always seem a petty realm to him. Then later, from many gentlemen, both French and Italian, I heard much about his noble manners, the greatness of his spirit, his valor and liberality; and I was told, among other things, how he loved and esteemed letters and how he held all men of letters in the greatest honor; and how he condemned the French themselves for being so hostile to this profession, especially as they have in their midst a university such as that of Paris, frequented by the whole world."

Then the Count said: "It is a great wonder that, at such a tender age, and solely by natural instinct and against the custom of his country, he should of himself have chosen so worthy a path; and, since subjects always imitate the ways of their superiors, it could be, as you say, that the French will yet come to esteem letters at their true worth: which they can easily be persuaded to do if they will but listen to reason, since nothing is more naturally desired by men or more proper to them than knowledge, and it is great folly to say or believe that knowledge is not always a good thing.

"And if I could speak with them or with others who hold an opinion contrary to mine, I would try to show them how useful and necessary to our life and dignity letters are, being truly bestowed upon men by God as a crowning gift; nor should I lack instances of many excellent commanders in antiquity, who all added the ornament of letters to valor in arms. For, as you know, Alexander venerated Homer so much that he always kept the *Iliad* by his bed. And he gave the greatest attention not only to these studies but to philosophical speculations as well, under Aristotle's guidance. Alcibiades increased his own good qualities and made them greater through letters and the teachings of Socrates. Also the effort that Caesar devoted to study is witnessed by the surviving works he so divinely wrote. Scipio Africanus, it is said, always kept in his hand the works of Xenophon, wherein, under the name of Cyrus, a perfect king is imagined. I could tell you of Lucullus, Sulla, Pompey, Brutus, and many other Romans and Greeks; but I will only remind you that Hannibal, so excellent a military commander, and yet fierce by nature and a stranger to all humanity, faithless and a despiser of men and the gods—had nonetheless some knowledge of letters and was conversant with Greek. And, if I am not mistaken, I think I once read that he even left a book written by him in Greek.

"But there is no need to tell you this, for I am sure you all know how mistaken the French are in thinking that letters are detrimental to arms. You know that the true stimulus to great and daring deeds in war is glory, and whosoever is moved thereto for gain or any other motive, apart from the fact that he never does anything good, deserves to be called not a gentleman, but a base merchant. And it is true glory that is entrusted to the sacred treasury of letters, as all may understand except those unhappy ones who have never tasted them.

"What soul is so abject, timid, and humble that when he reads of the great deeds of Caesar, Alexander, Scipio, Hannibal, and many others, does not burn with a most ardent desire to resemble them, and does not reckon this transitory life of a few days' span as less important, in order to win to an almost eternal life of fame which, in spite of death, makes him live on in far greater glory than before. But he who does not taste the sweetness of letters cannot know how great the glory is that letters so long preserve, and measures it only by the life of one or two men, because his own memory extends no further. Hence, he cannot value so brief a glory as he would one that is almost eternal (if, to his misfortune, he were not denied knowledge of it); and since he does not much esteem it, we may with reason think that he will not risk such danger to win it as one would who knows of it.

"But I should not want some objector to cite me instances to the contrary in order to refute my opinion, alleging that for all their knowledge of letters the Italians have shown little worth in arms for some time now—which, alas, is only too true. But it must be said that the fault of a few men has brought not only serious harm but eternal blame upon all the rest, and that they have been the true cause of our ruin and of the prostrate (if not dead) virtue of our spirits. Yet it would be a greater shame if we made this fact public than it is to the French to be ignorant of letters. Hence, it is better to pass over in silence what cannot be remembered without pain: and, leaving this subject, upon which I entered against my will, to return to our Courtier.

"I would have him more than passably learned in letters, at least in those studies which we call the humanities. Let him be conversant not only with the Latin language, but with Greek as well, because of the abundance and variety of things that are so divinely written therein. Let him be versed in the poets, as well as in the orators and historians, and let him be practiced also in writing verse and prose, especially in our own vernacular; for, beside the personal satisfaction he will take in this, in this way he will never want for pleasant entertainment with the ladies, who are usually fond of such things. And if, because of other occupations or lack of study, he does not attain to such a perfection that his writings should merit great praise, let him take care to keep them under cover so that others will not laugh at him, and let him show them only to a friend who can be trusted; because at least they will be of profit to him in that, through such exercise, he will be capable of judging the writing of others. For it very rarely happens that a man who is unpracticed in writing, however learned he may be, can ever wholly understand the toils and industry of writers, or taste the sweetness and excellence of styles, and those intrinsic niceties that are often found in the ancients.

These studies, moreover, will make him fluent, and (as Aristippus said to the tyrant) bold and self-confident in speaking with everyone. However, I would have our Courtier keep one precept firmly in mind, namely, in this as in everything else, to be cautious and reserved rather than forward, and take care not to get the mistaken notion that he knows something he does not know. For we are all by nature more avid of praise than we ought to be and, more than any other sweet song or sound, our ears love the melody of words that praise us; and thus, like Sirens' voices, they are the cause of shipwreck to him who does not stop his ears to such beguiling harmony. This danger was recognized by the ancients, and books were written to show how the true friend is to be distinguished from the flatterer. But to what avail is this, if many, indeed countless persons know full well when they are being flattered, yet love the one who flatters them and hate the one who tells them the truth? And finding him who praises them to be too sparing in his words, they even help him and proceed to say such things of themselves that they make the impudent flatterer himself feel ashamed.

"Let us leave these blind ones to their error, and let us have our Courtier be of such good judgment that he will not let himself be persuaded that black is white, or presume of himself more than he clearly knows to be true; and especially in those points which (if your memory serves you) Messer Cesare said we had often used as the means of bringing to light the folly of many persons. Indeed, even if he knows that the praises bestowed upon him are true, let him avoid error by not assenting too openly to them, nor concede them without some protest; but let him rather disclaim them modestly, always showing and really esteeming arms as his chief profession, and the other good accomplishments as ornaments thereto; and do this especially when among soldiers, in order not to act like those who in studies wish to appear as soldiers, and, when in the company of warriors, wish to appear as men of letters. In this way, for the reasons we have stated, he will avoid affection and even the ordinary things he does will appear to be very great things."

Messer Pietro Bembo[1] replied: "Count, I do not see why you insist that this Courtier, who is lettered and who has so many other worthy qualities, should regard everything as an ornament of arms, and not regard arms and the rest as an ornament of letters; which,

[1] See the selection from Bembo's *Gli Asolani*, reprinted above.

without any other accompaniment, are as superior to arms in worth
as the soul is to the body, because the practice of them pertains
properly to the soul, even as that of arms does to the body."

Then the Count replied: "Nay, the practice of arms pertains to
both the soul and the body. But I would not have you be a judge in
such a case, Messer Pietro, because you would be too much suspected
of bias by one of the parties. And as this is a debate that has long
been waged by very wise men, there is no need to renew it; but I
consider it decided in favor of arms; and since I may form our
Courtier as I please, I would have him be of the same opinion. And
if you are contrary-minded, wait until you can hear of a contest
wherein the one who defends the cause of arms is permitted to use
arms, just as those who defend letters make use of letters in defending their own cause; for if everyone avails himself of his own
weapons, you will see that the men of letters will lose."

"Ah," said Messer Pietro, "a while ago you damned the French
for their slight appreciation of letters, and you spoke of what a
light of glory letters shed on a man, how they make him immortal;
and now it appears that you have changed your mind. Do you not
remember that

> *Giunto Alessandro alla famosa tomba*
> *del fero Achille, sospirando disse:*
> *"O fortunato, che si chiara tromba*
> *trovasti, e chi di te si alto scrisse!"*

When Alexander had come to the famous tomb of Achilles, sighing, he
said: 'O fortunate man, to find so clear a trumpet and someone to
write of you so loftily!'

And if Alexander envied Achilles, not for his exploits, but for the
fortune which had granted him the blessing of having his deeds
celebrated by Homer, we see that he esteemed Homer's letters
above Achilles' arms. What other judge would you have, or what
other sentence on the worthiness of arms and of letters than what
has been pronounced by one of the greatest commanders that have
ever been?"

Then the Count replied: "I blame the French for thinking that
letters are detrimental to the profession of arms, and I hold that to

no one is learning more suited than to a warrior; and I would have these two accomplishments conjoined in our Courtier, each an aid to the other, as is most fitting: nor do I think I have changed my opinion in this. But, as I said, I do not wish to argue as to which of the two is more deserving of praise. Let it suffice to say that men of letters almost never choose to praise any save great men and glorious deeds, which in themselves deserve praise because of the essential worthiness from which they derive; beside this, such men and deeds are very noble material for writers, and are in themselves a great ornament and partly the reason why such writing is perpetuated, which perhaps would not be so much read or prized if it lacked a noble subject, but would be empty and of little moment.

"And if Alexander envied Achilles for being praised by Homer, this does not prove that he esteemed letters more than arms; wherein if he had thought himself to be as far beneath Achilles as he deemed all those who were to write of him to be beneath Homer, I am certain that he would have much preferred fine deeds on his own part to fine talk on the part of others. Hence, I believe that what he said was tacit praise of himself, expressing a desire for what he thought he lacked, namely, the supreme excellence of some writer, and not for what he believed he had already attained, namely, prowess in arms, wherein he did not at all take Achilles to be his superior. Wherefore he called him fortunate, as though to suggest that if his own fame had hitherto not been so celebrated in the world as Achilles' had (which was made bright and illustrious by a poem so divine), this was not because his valor and merits were fewer or less deserving of praise, but because Fortune had granted Achilles such a miracle of nature to be the glorious trumpet for his deeds. Perhaps he wished also to incite some noble talent to write about him, thereby showing that his pleasure in this would be as great as his love and veneration for the sacred monuments of letters: about which by now we have said quite enough."

"Nay, too much," replied signor Ludovico Pio, "for I believe it is not possible in all the world to find a vessel large enough to contain all the things you would have be in our Courtier."

Then the Count said: "Wait a little, for there are yet many more to come. . . ."

℀ LEONARDO DA VINCI

Leonardo, the illegitimate son of a Florentine lawyer, was born in 1452 at Vinci, a village in Tuscany. In 1519 he died in France, an honored member of the court of Francis I. He was a legend in his own time, not only for his unbounded curiosity, energy, and brilliance, but also for his great charm and his unusual physical beauty. Leonardo became, in the course of his life, one of the most accomplished men of the Renaissance, and perhaps of all time, in the arts of painting, sculpture, drawing, and architecture, as well as in engineering, mechanics, hydraulics, anatomy, and philosophy.

At eighteen, Leonardo was apprenticed in the studio of Andrea del Verrocchio, where he remained until 1477, by which time he had mastered the visual arts. He stayed in Florence for some years thereafter, perfecting the naturalistic techniques of painting which, in only a handful of surviving works, have aroused wonder and admiration ever since. In 1483 he joined the court of Ludovico Sforza at Milan, where he developed many practical, and some visionary plans to improve the fortifications, sanitation, architecture, and civic art of the city. His almost incredible versatility found expression here in dozens of bold projects, not the least of which was the *Last Supper* (1494-98), a fresco painted in the refectory of Santa Maria delle Grazie.

Leonardo's *Notebooks* offer the most precious and precise information concerning the details of his thought. Originally written in his enigmatic mirror-writing, without any system of organization, over a period of decades, the manuscripts have suffered many changes for the worse since his death. Yet the texts that survive, with the hundreds of drawings that accompany them, reveal in many ways Leonardo's incomparable

163

artistic and scientific powers, the depth and scope of his intellect, his sensibility, even his humor. In the selections that follow, his thoughts on philosophy, mathematics, nature, and the arts have been arranged topically with no concern for chronological order. They offer interesting implicit points of comparison and contrast with the views and methods of Castiglione, Pico, and Machiavelli. (From *The Notebooks of Leonardo da Vinci,* edited by Edward MacCurdy. New York: George Braziller, Inc., 1958, pp. 57-59, 61-66, 81-85, 852-56, 902-3. Reprinted by permission of George Braziller, Inc.)

From Leonardo's *Notebooks*
Proem

If indeed I have no power to quote from authors as they have, it is a far bigger and more worthy thing to read by the light of experience, which is the instructress of their masters. They strut about puffed up and pompous, decked out and adorned not with their own labors but by those of others, and they will not even allow me my own. And if they despise me who am an inventor how much more should blame be given to themselves, who are not inventors but trumpeters and reciters of the works of others?

* * *

Those who are inventors and interpreters between Nature and Man as compared with the reciters and trumpeters of the works of others, are to be considered simply as is an object in front of a mirror in comparison with its image when seen in the mirror, the one being something in itself, the other nothing: people whose debt to nature is small, for it seems only by chance that they wear human form, and but for this one might class them with the herds of beasts.

Seeing that I cannot choose any subject of great utility or pleasure, because my predecessors have already taken as their own all useful and necessary themes, I will do like one who, because of his poverty, is the last to arrive at the fair, and not being able otherwise to provide himself, chooses all things which others have already looked over and not taken, but refused as being of little value. With these despised and rejected wares—the leavings of many buyers—I will load my modest pack, and therewith take my course, distributing, not indeed amid the great cities, but among the mean hamlets, and taking such reward as befits the things I offer.

I am fully aware that the fact of my not being a man of letters may cause certain arrogant persons to think that they may with reason censure me, alleging that I am a man ignorant of book-learning. Foolish folk! Do they not know that I might retort by saying, as did Marius to the Roman Patricians: "They who themselves go about adorned in the labor of others will not permit me my own"? They will say that because of my lack of book-learning I cannot properly express what I desire to treat of. Do they not know that my subjects require for their exposition experience rather than the words of others? And since experience has been the mistress of whoever has written well, I take her as my mistress, and to her in all points make my appeal.

Many will believe that they can with reason censure me, alleging that my proofs are contrary to the authority of certain men who are held in great reverence by their inexperienced judgments, not taking into account that my conclusions were arrived at as a result of simple and plain experience, which is the true mistress.

These rules enable you to discern the true from the false, and thus to set before yourselves only things possible and of more moderation; and they forbid you to use a cloak of ignorance, which will bring about that you attain to no result and in despair abandon yourself to melancholy.

The natural desire of good men is knowledge.

I know that many will call this a useless work, and they will be those of whom Demetrius said that he took no more account of the wind that produced the words in their mouths than of the wind that came out of their hinder parts: men whose only desire is for material riches and luxury and who are entirely destitute of the desire of wisdom, the sustenance and the only true riches of the soul. For as the soul is more worthy than the body so much are the soul's riches more worthy than those of the body. And often when I see one of these men take this work in hand I wonder whether he will not put it to his nose like the ape, and ask me whether it is something to eat.

Begun in Florence in the house of Piero di Braccio Martelli, on the 22nd day of March, 1508. This will be a collection without order, made up of many sheets which I have copied here, hoping afterward to arrange them in order in their proper places according to the subjects of which they treat; and I believe that before I am at the end of this I shall have to repeat the same thing several times; and therefore, O reader, blame me not, because the subjects are many, and the memory cannot retain them and say "this I will not write because I have already written it." And if I wished to avoid falling into this mistake it would be necessary, in order to prevent repetition, that on every occasion when I wished to transcribe a passage I should always read over all the preceding portion, and this especially because long periods of time elapse between one time of writing and another. . . .

Philosophy

"Nature is full of infinite causes which were never set forth in experience."

We have no lack of system or device to measure and to parcel out these poor days of ours; wherein it should be our pleasure that they be not squandered or suffered to pass away in vain, and without meed of honor, leaving no record of themselves in the minds of men; to the end that this our poor course may not be sped in vain.

Our judgment does not reckon in their exact and proper order things which have come to pass at different periods of time; for many things which happened many years ago will seem nearly related to the present, and many things that are recent will seem ancient, extending back to the far-off period of our youth. And so it is with the eye, with regard to distant things, which when illumined by the sun seem near to the eye, while many things which are near seem far off.

Supreme happiness will be the greatest cause of misery, and the perfection of wisdom the occasion of folly.

Every part is disposed to unite with the whole, that it may thereby escape from its own incompleteness.

The soul desires to dwell with the body because without the members of that body it can neither act nor feel. . . .

O Time, thou that consumest all things! O envious age, thou destroyest all things and devourest all things with the hard teeth of the years, little by little, in slow death! Helen, when she looked in her mirror and saw the withered wrinkles which old age had made in her face, wept, and wondered to herself why ever she had twice been carried away.

O Time, thou that consumest all things! O envious age, whereby all things are consumed!

The age as it flies glides secretly and deceives one and another; nothing is more fleeting than the years, but he who sows virtue reaps honor.

Wrongfully do men lament the flight of time, accusing it of being too swift, and not perceiving that its period is yet sufficient; but good memory wherewith Nature has endowed us causes everything long past to seem present.

Whoever would see in what state the soul dwells within the body, let him mark how this body uses its daily habitation, for if this be confused and without order the body will be kept in disorder and confusion by the soul.

O thou that sleepest, what is sleep? Sleep is an image of death. Oh, why not let your work be such that after death you become an image of immortality; as in life you become when sleeping like unto the hapless dead.

Man and the animals are merely a passage and channel for food, a tomb for other animals, a haven for the dead, giving life by the death of others, a coffer full of corruption.

Behold a thing which the more need there is of it is the more rejected: this is advice, listened to unwillingly by those who have most need of it, that is by the ignorant. Behold a thing which the more you have fear of it and the more you flee from it comes the nearer to you: this is misery, which the more you flee from it makes you the more wretched and without rest.

Experience, the interpreter between resourceful nature and the human species, teaches that that which this nature works out among mortals constrained by necessity cannot operate in any other way than that in which reason which is its rudder teaches it to work.

To the ambitious, whom neither the boon of life nor the beauty of the world suffice to content, it comes as penance that life with them is squandered, and that they possess neither the benefits nor the beauty of the world.

The air as soon as there is light is filled with innumerable images to which the eye serves as a magnet.

In youth acquire that which may requite you for the deprivations of old age; and if you are mindful that old age has wisdom for its food you will so exert yourself in youth that your old age will not lack sustenance.

There is no result in nature without a cause; understand the cause and you will have no need of the experiment.

Experience is never at fault; it is only your judgment that is in error in promising itself such results from experience as are not caused by our experiments. For having given a beginning, what follows from it must necessarily be a natural development of such a beginning, unless it has been subject to a contrary influence, while, if it is affected by any contrary influence, the result which ought to follow from the aforesaid beginning will be found to partake of this contrary influence in a greater or less degree in proportion as the said influence is more or less powerful than the aforesaid beginning.

Experience is not at fault; it is only our judgment that is in error in promising itself from experience things which are not within her power.

Wrongly do men cry out against experience and with bitter reproaches accuse her of deceitfulness. Let experience alone, and rather turn your complaints against your own ignorance, which causes you to be so carried away by your vain and insensate desires as to expect from experience things which are not within her power!

Wrongly do men cry out against innocent experience, accusing her often of deceit and lying demonstrations!

O mathematicians, throw light on this error.

The spirit has no voice, for where there is voice there is a body, and where there is a body there is occupation of space which prevents the eye from seeing things situated beyond this space; consequently this body of itself fills the whole surrounding air, that is by its images.

The body of the earth is of the nature of a fish, a grampus or sperm whale, because it draws water as its breath instead of air.

How the movements of the eye, of the ray of the sun, and of the mind are the swiftest that can be:

The sun so soon as ever it appears in the east instantly proceeds with its rays to the west; and these are made up of three incorporeal forces, namely radiance, heat, and the image of the shape which produces these.

The eye so soon as ever it is opened beholds all the stars of our hemisphere.

The mind passes in an instant from the east to the west; and all the great incorporeal things resemble these very closely in their speed.

When you wish to produce a result by means of an instrument do not allow yourself to complicate it by introducing many subsidiary parts but follow the briefest way possible, and do not act as those do who when they do not know how to express a thing in its own proper vocabulary proceed by a method of circumlocution and with great prolixity and confusion.

Two weaknesses leaning together create a strength. Therefore the half of the world leaning against the other half becomes firm.

While I thought that I was learning how to live, I have been learning how to die.

Every part of an element separated from its mass desires to return to it by the shortest way.

Nothingness has no center, and its boundaries are nothingness.

My opponent says that nothingness and a vacuum are one and the same thing, having indeed two separate names by which they are called, but not existing separately in nature.

The reply is that whenever there exists a vacuum there will also be the space which surrounds it, but nothingness exists apart from occupation of space; it follows that nothingness and a vacuum are not the same, for the one is divisible to infinity, and nothingness cannot be divided because nothing can be less than it is; and if you were to take part from it this part would be equal to the whole, and the whole to the part.

Aristotle in the Third [Book] of the *Ethics:* man is worthy of praise and blame solely in respect of such actions as it is within his power to do or to abstain from.

He who expects from experience what she does not possess takes leave of reason.

For what reason do such animals as sow their seed sow with pleasure and the one who awaits receives with pleasure and brings forth with pain?

Intellectual passion drives out sensuality.

The knowledge of past time and of the position of the earth is the adornment and the food of human minds.

Among the great things which are found among us the existence of Nothing is the greatest. This dwells in time, and stretches its limbs into the past and the future, and with these takes to itself all works that are past and those that are to come, both of nature and of the animals, and possesses nothing of the indivisible present. It does not however extend to the essence of anything. . . .

OF NECROMANCY

But of all human discourses that must be considered as most foolish which affirms a belief in necromancy, which is the sister of alchemy, the producer of simple and natural things, but is so much the more worthy of blame than alchemy, because it never gives birth to anything whatever except to things like itself, that is to say lies; and this is not the case with alchemy, which works by the simple products of nature, but whose function cannot be exercised by nature herself, because there are in her no organic instruments with which she might be able to do the work which man performs with his hands, by the use of which he has made glass, etc. But this necromancy, an ensign or flying banner, blown by the wind, is the guide of the foolish multitude, which is a continual witness by its clamor to the limitless effects of such an art. And they have filled whole books in affirming that enchantments and spirits can work and speak without tongues, and can speak without any organic instrument—without which speech is impossible—and can carry the heaviest weights, and bring tempests and rain, and that men can be changed into cats and wolves and other beasts, although those first become beasts who affirm such things.

And undoubtedly if this necromancy did exist, as is believed by shallow minds, there is nothing on earth that would have so much power either to harm or to benefit man; if it were true, that is, that by such an art one had the power to disturb the tranquil clearness of the air, and transform it into the hue of night, to create coruscations and tempests with dreadful thunder-claps and lightning-flashes rushing through the darkness, and with impetuous storms to overthrow high buildings and uproot forests, and with these to encounter armies and break and overthrow them, and—more important even than this—to make the devastating tempests, and thereby rob the husbandmen of the reward of their labors. For what method of warfare can there be which can inflict such damage upon the enemy as the exercise of the power to deprive him of his crops? What naval combat could there be which should compare with that which he would wage who has command of the winds and can create ruinous tempests that would submerge every fleet whatsoever? In truth, whoever has control of such irresistible forces will be lord over all nations, and no human skill will be able to resist his destructive power. The buried treasures, the jewels that lie in the body of the earth will all become manifest to him; no lock, no fortress, however impregnable, will avail to save anyone against the will of such a necromancer. He will cause himself to be carried through the air from east to west, and through all the uttermost parts of the universe. But why do I thus go on adding instance to instance? What is there which could not be brought to pass by a mechanician such as this? Almost nothing, except the escaping from death.

We have therefore ascertained in part the mischief and the usefulness that belong to such an art if it is real; and if it is real why has it not remained among men who desire so much, not having regard to any deity, merely because there are an infinite number of persons who in order to gratify one of their appetites would destroy God and the whole universe?

If then it has never remained among men, although so necessary to them, it never existed, and never can exist, as follows from the definition of a spirit, which is invisible and incorporeal, for within the elements there are no incorporeal things, because where there is not body there is a vacuum, and the vacuum does not exist within the elements, because it would be instantly filled up by the element.

Therefore O students study mathematics and do not build without foundations.

Mental things which have not passed through the understanding are vain and give birth to no truth other than what is harmful. And because such discourses spring from poverty of intellect those who make them are always poor, and if they have been born rich they shall die poor in their old age. For nature, as it would seem, takes vengeance on such as would work miracles and they come to have less than other men who are more quiet. And those who wish to grow rich in a day shall live a long time in great poverty, as happens and will to all eternity happen to the alchemists, the would-be creators of gold and silver, and to the engineers who think to make dead water stir itself into life with perpetual motion, and to those supreme fools, the necromancer and the enchanter.

[THE CERTAINTY OF MATHEMATICS]

He who blames the supreme certainty of mathematics feeds on confusion, and will never impose silence upon the contradictions of the sophistical sciences, which occasion a perpetual clamor.

The abbreviators of works do injury to knowledge and to love, for love of anything is the offspring of knowledge, love being more fervent in proportion as knowledge is more certain; and this certainty springs from a thorough knowledge of all those parts which united compose the whole of that thing which ought to be loved.

Of what use, pray, is he who in order to abridge the part of the things of which he professes to give complete information leaves out the greater part of the matters of which the whole is composed?

True it is that impatience, the mother of folly, is she who praises brevity; as though such folk had not a span of life that would suffice to acquire complete knowledge of one particular subject such as the human body. And then they think to comprehend the mind of God which embraces the whole universe, weighing and dissecting it as though they were making an anatomy. O human stupidity! Do you not perceive that you have spent your whole life with yourself and yet are not aware of that which you have most in evidence, and that is your own foolishness? And so with the crowd of sophists you think to deceive yourself and others, despising the mathematical sciences in which is contained true information about the subjects of which they treat! Or you would fain range among the miracles and give your views upon those subjects which the human mind is incapable of comprehending and which cannot be demonstrated by any natural instance. And it seems to you that you have performed miracles when you have spoiled the work of some ingenious mind, and you do not perceive that you are falling into the same error as does he who strips a tree of its adornment of branches laden with leaves intermingled with fragrant flowers or fruits, in order to demonstrate the suitability of the tree for making planks. Even as did Justinus, maker of an epitome of the histories of Trogus Pompeius, who had written an elaborate account of all the great deeds of his ancestors which lent themselves to picturesque description, for by so doing he composed a bald work fit only for such impatient minds as conceive themselves to be wasting time when they spend it usefully in study of the works of nature and of human things.

Let such as these remain in the company of the beasts, and let their courtiers be dogs and other animals eager for prey and let them keep company with them; ever pursuing whatever takes flight from them, they follow after the inoffensive animals who in the season of the snow drifts are impelled by hunger to approach your doors to beg alms from you as from a guardian.

If you are as you have described yourself, the king of the animals —it would be better for you to call yourself king of the beasts since you are the greatest of them all!—why do you not help them so that they may presently be able to give you their young in order to gratify your palate, for the sake of which you have tried to make yourself a tomb for all the animals? Even more I might say if to speak the entire truth were permitted me.

But do not let us quit this subject without referring to one supreme form of wickedness which hardly exists among the animals, among whom are none that devour their own species except for lack of reason (for there are insane among them as among human beings though not in such great numbers). Nor does this happen except among the voracious animals as in the lion species and among leopards, panthers, lynxes, cats, and creatures like these, which sometimes eat their young. But not only do you eat your children, but you eat father, mother, brothers, and friends; and this even not sufficing you, you make raids on foreign islands and capture men of other races and then, after mutilating them in a shameful manner, you fatten them up and cram them down your gullet. Say does not nature bring forth a sufficiency of simple things to produce satiety? Or if you cannot content yourself with simple things can you not by blending these together make an infinite number of compounds as did Platina and other authors who have written for epicures?

And if any be found virtuous and good drive them not away from you but do them honor lest they flee from you and take refuge in hermitages and caves or other solitary places in order to escape from your deceits. If any such be found, pay him reverence, for as these are as gods upon the earth they deserve statues, images, and honors. But I would impress upon you that their images are not to be eaten by you, as happens in a certain district of India; for there, when in the judgment of the priests these images have worked some miracle, they cut them in pieces being of wood and distribute them to all the people of the locality—not without payment.

And each of them then grates his portion very fine and spreads it over the first food he eats; and so they consider that symbolically by faith they have eaten their saint, and they believe that he will then guard them from all dangers. What think you Man! of your species? Are you as wise as you set yourself up to be? Are acts such as these things that men should do, Justinus?

Let no one read me who is not a mathematician in my beginnings.

Every action of nature is made alone the shortest possible way.

Thou, O God, dost sell unto us all good things at the price of labour. . . .

Comparison of the Arts

"If you know how to describe and write down the appearance of the forms, the painter can make them so that they appear enlivened with lights and shadows which create the very expression of the faces; herein you cannot attain with the pen where he attains with the brush."

How painting surpasses all human works by reason of the subtle possibilities which it contains:

The eye, which is called the window of the soul, is the chief means whereby the understanding may most fully and abundantly appreciate the infinite works of nature; and the ear is the second, inasmuch as it acquires its importance from the fact that it hears the things which the eye has seen. If you historians, or poets, or mathematicians had never seen things with your eyes you would be ill able to describe them in your writings. And if you, O poet, represent a story by depicting it with your pen, the painter with his brush will so render it as to be more easily satisfying and less tedious to understand. If you call painting "dumb poetry," then the painter may say of the poet that his art is "blind painting." Consider then which is the more grievous affliction, to be blind or to be dumb! Although the poet has as wide a choice of subjects as the painter, his creations fail to afford as much satisfaction to mankind as do paintings, for while poetry attempts to represent forms, actions, and scenes with words, the painter employs the exact images of these forms in order to reproduce them. Consider, then, which is more fundamental to man, the name of man or his image? The name changes with change of country; the form is unchanged except by death.

And if the poet serves the understanding by way of the ear, the painter does so by the eye, which is the nobler sense.

I will only cite as an instance of this how if a good painter represents the fury of a battle and a poet also describes one, and the

two descriptions are shown together to the public, you will soon
see which will draw most of the spectators, and where there will be
most discussion, to which most praise will be given, and which will
satisfy the more. There is no doubt that the painting, which is by
far the more useful and beautiful, will give the greater pleasure.
Inscribe in any place the name of God and set opposite to it His
image, you will see which will be held in greater reverence!

Since painting embraces within itself all the forms of nature, you
have omitted nothing except the names, and these are not universal
like the forms. If you have the results of her processes we have the
processes of her results.

Take the case of a poet describing the beauties of a lady to her
lover and that of a painter who makes a portrait of her; you will
see whither nature will the more incline the enamoured judge.
Surely the proof of the matter ought to rest upon the verdict of
experience!

You have set painting among the mechanical arts! Truly, were
painters as ready equipped as you are to praise their own works in
writing, I doubt whether it would endure the reproach of so vile a
name. If you call it mechanical because it is by manual work that
the hands represent what the imagination creates, your writers are
setting down with the pen by manual work what originates in the
mind. If you call it mechanical because it is done for money, who
fall into this error—if indeed it can be called an error—more than
you yourselves? If you lecture for the schools do you not go to whoever pays you the most? Do you do any work without some reward?

And yet I do not say this in order to censure such opinions, for
every labor looks for its reward. And if the poet should say, "I will
create a fiction which shall express great things," so likewise will the
painter also, for even so Apelles made the Calumny. If you should
say that poetry is the more enduring—to this I would reply that the
works of a coppersmith are more enduring still, since time preserves
them longer than either your works or ours; nevertheless they show
but little imagination; and painting, if it be done upon copper in
enamel colors, can be made far more enduring.

In Art we may be said to be grandsons unto God. If poetry treats
of moral philosophy, painting has to do with natural philosophy;
if the one describes the workings of the mind, the other considers

what the mind effects by movements of the body; if the one dismays folk by hellish fictions, the other does the like by showing the same things in action. Suppose the poet sets himself to represent some image of beauty or terror, something vile and foul, or some monstrous thing, in contest with the painter, and suppose in his own way he makes a change of forms at his pleasure, will not the painter still satisfy the more? Have we not seen pictures which bear so close a resemblance to the actual thing that they have deceived both men and beasts?

If you know how to describe and write down the appearance of the forms, the painter can make them so that they appear enlivened with lights and shadows which create the very expression of the faces; herein you cannot attain with the pen where he attains with the brush.

How he who despises painting has no love for the philosophy in nature:

If you despise painting, which is the sole imitator of all the visible works of nature, it is certain that you will be despising a subtle invention which with philosophical and ingenious speculation takes as its theme all the various kinds of forms, airs and scenes, plants, animals, grasses and flowers, which are surrounded by light and shade. And this truly is a science and the true-born daughter of nature, since painting is the offspring of nature. But in order to speak more correctly we may call it the grandchild of nature; for all visible things derive their existence from nature, and from these same things is born painting. So therefore we may justly speak of it as the grandchild of nature and as related to God himself.

That sculpture is less intellectual than painting, and lacks many of its natural parts:

As practising myself the art of sculpture no less than that of painting, and doing both the one and the other in the same degree, it seems to me that without suspicion of unfairness I may venture to give an opinion as to which of the two is the more intellectual, and of the greater difficulty and perfection.

In the first place, sculpture is dependent on certain lights, namely those from above, while a picture carries everywhere with it its own light and shade; light and shade therefore are essential to sculpture. In this respect, the sculptor is aided by the nature of the relief, which produces these of its own accord, but the painter artificially creates them by his art in places where nature would normally do the like. The sculptor cannot render the difference in the varying natures of the colors of objects; painting does not fail to do so in any particular. The lines of perspective of sculptors do not seem in any way true; those of painters may appear to extend a hundred miles beyond the work itself. The effects of aerial perspective are outside the scope of sculptors' work; they can neither represent transparent bodies nor luminous bodies nor angles of reflection nor shining bodies such as mirrors and like things of glittering surface, nor mists, nor dull weather, nor an infinite number of things which I forbear to mention lest they should prove wearisome.

The one advantage which sculpture has is that of offering greater resistance to time; yet painting offers a like resistance if it is done upon thick copper covered with white enamel and then painted upon with enamel colors and placed in a fire and fused. In degree of permanence it then surpasses even sculpture.

It may be urged that if a mistake is made it is not easy to set it right, but it is a poor line of argument to attempt to prove that the fact of a mistake being irremediable makes the work more noble. I should say indeed that it is more difficult to correct the mind of the master who makes such mistakes than the work which he has spoiled.

We know very well that a good experienced painter will not make such mistakes; on the contrary, following sound rules he will proceed by removing so little at a time that his work will progress well. The sculptor also if he is working in clay or wax can either take away from it or add to it, and when the model is completed it is easy to cast it in bronze; and this is the last process and it is the most enduring form of sculpture, since that which is only in marble is liable to be destroyed, but not when done in bronze.

But painting done upon copper, which by the methods in use in painting may be either taken from or altered, is like the bronze, for when you have first made the model for this in wax it can still be either reduced or altered. While the sculpture in bronze is imperishable this painting upon copper and enamelling is absolutely eternal; and while bronze remains dark and rough, this is full of an infinite variety of varied and lovely colors, of which I have already made mention. But if you would have me speak only of panel painting I am content to give an opinion between it and sculpture by saying that painting is more beautiful, more imaginative, and richer in resource, while sculpture is more enduring, but excels in nothing else.

Sculpture reveals what it is with little effort; painting seems a thing miraculous, making things intangible appear tangible, presenting in relief things which are flat, in distance things near at hand.

In fact, painting is adorned with infinite possibilities of which sculpture can make no use.

One of the chief proofs of skill of the painter is that his picture should seem in relief, and this is not the case with the sculptor, for in this respect he is aided by nature.

[OF POETRY AND PAINTING]

When the poet ceases to represent in words what exists in nature, he then ceases to be the equal of the painter; for if the poet, leaving such representation, were to describe the polished and persuasive words of one whom he wishes to represent as speaking, he would be becoming an orator and be no more a poet or a painter. And if he were to describe the heavens he makes himself an astrologer, and a philosopher or theologian when speaking of the things of nature or of God. But if he returns to the representation of some definite thing he would become the equal of the painter if he could satisfy the eye with words as the painter does with brush and color, [for with these he creates] a harmony to the eye, even as music does in an instant to the ear.

[PAINTING AND SCULPTURE]

Why the picture seen with two eyes will not be an example of such relief as the relief seen with two eyes; this is because the picture seen with one eye will place itself in relief like the actual relief, having the same qualities of light and shade. . . .

How from age to age the art of painting continually declines and deteriorates when painters have no other standard than work already done:

The painter will produce pictures of little merit if he takes the works of others as his standard; but if he will apply himself to learn from the objects of nature he will produce good results. This we see was the case with the painters who came after the time of the Romans, for they continually imitated each other, and from age to age their art steadily declined.

After these came Giotto the Florentine, and he—reared in mountain solitudes, inhabited only by goats and such like beasts— turning straight from nature to his art, began to draw on the rocks the movements of the goats which he was tending, and so began to draw the figures of all the animals which were to be found in the country, in such a way that after much study he not only surpassed the masters of his own time but all those of many preceding centuries. After him art again declined, because all were imitating paintings already done; and so for centuries it continued to decline until such time as Tommaso the Florentine, nicknamed Masaccio, showed by the perfection of his work how those who took as their standard anything other than nature, the supreme guide of all the masters, were wearying themselves in vain. Similarly I would say about these mathematical subjects, that those who study only the authorities and not the works of nature are in art the grandsons and not the sons of nature, which is the supreme guide of the good authorities.

Mark the supreme folly of those who censure such as learn from nature, leaving uncensured the authorities who were themselves the disciples of this same nature!

READING LIST

C. M. Ady, *Lorenzo de'Medici and Renaissance Italy*. New York: The Crowell-Collier Publishing Co.

H. Baron, *The Crisis of the Early Italian Renaissance*, 2 vols. Princeton: Princeton University Press, 1955.

R. R. Bolgar, *The Classical Heritage and its Beneficiaries*. Cambridge: Cambridge University Press, 1954.

J. Burckhardt, *The Civilization of the Renaissance in Italy*, tr. Middlemore. Many editions.

E. Cassirer, *The Individual and the Cosmos in Renaissance Philosophy*, tr. Mario Domandi. New York: Harper Torchbooks.

*F. Chabod, *Machiavelli and the Renaissance*. Cambridge, Mass.: Harvard University Press, 1958.

W. K. Ferguson, *Europe in Transition, 1300-1520*. Cambridge, Mass.: Houghton Mifflin Co., 1963.

—————, *The Renaissance in Historical Thought*. Cambridge, Mass.: Houghton Mifflin Co., 1948.

D. J. Geanakoplos, *Greek Scholars in Venice*. Cambridge, Mass.: Harvard University Press, 1962.

*M. P. Gilmore, *The World of Humanism, 1453-1517*. New York: Harper & Row, 1952.

J. R. Hale, *Machiavelli and Renaissance Italy*. New York: The Crowell-Collier Publishing Co.

D. Hay, *The Italian Renaissance in its Historical Background*. Cambridge: Cambridge University Press, 1961.

P. O. Kristeller, *Renaissance Thought*, 2 vols. New York: Harper Torchbooks, 1961 and 1964.

—————, *Eight Philosophers of the Italian Renaissance*. Stanford: Stanford University Press, 1964.

A. von Martin, *The Sociology of the Renaissance*. New York: Harper Torchbooks.

* Contain useful bibliographies.

L. Martines, *The Social World of the Florentine Humanists*. Princeton: Princeton University Press, 1963.

I. Origo, *The Merchant of Prato: Franceso di Marco Datini, 1335-1410*. New York: Alfred A. Knopf, Inc., 1957.

——————, *The World of San Bernardino*. New York: Harcourt, Brace & World, 1962.

E. Panofsky, *Studies in Iconology*. New York: Harper Torchbooks.

Eugene F. Rice, Jr., *The Renaissance Idea of Wisdom*. Cambridge, Mass.: Harvard University Press, 1958.

F. Schevill, *Medieval and Renaissance Florence*, 2 vols. New York: Harper Torchbooks.

B. L. Ullman, *The Humanism of Coluccio Salutati*. Padua: Ed. Antenore, 1963.